Shamanic Journeys, Shamanic Stories

Shamanic Journeys, Shamanic Stories

Michael Berman

BOOKS

Winchester, UK
Washington, USA

First published by O-Books, 2011
O Books is an imprint of John Hunt Publishing Ltd., The Bothy, Deershot Lodge, Park Lane, Ropley,
Hants, SO24 0BE, UK
office1@o-books.net
www.o-books.com

For distributor details and how to order please visit the 'Ordering' section on our website.

Text copyright: Michael Berman 2010

ISBN: 978 1 84694 402 4

A CIP catalogue record for this book is available from the British Library.

Design: Tom Davies

Printed in the UK by CPI Antony Rowe
Printed in the USA by Offset Paperback Mfrs, Inc

We operate a distinctive and ethical publishing philosophy in all
areas of its business, from its global network of authors to
production and worldwide distribution.

CONTENTS

Introduction: The Status of Shamanism Today

"[I]f indigenous religious perspectives continue to be ignored, or at least marginalized in academic circles, a highly significant portion of the world's religious adherents will be excluded from scholarly research and teaching in religious studies" (Cox, 2007, p.1).

To qualify as a world religion, a faith must in some sense be comparable to Christianity, either by possessing components that can be translated into Christian terms, like scriptures, doctrines or festivals, or by mounting a strenuous challenge to Christianity, such as occurred in the proselytizing activities of Islam or that became evident as Westerners encountered the intellectual sophistication of philosophical Hinduism. In each case, the 'success' of the 'non-Christian' religions elevated their status within Western renditions of history (Cox, 2007, p.47). However, Shamanism, like Wicca, is a non-scriptural faith. From this it becomes evident, if it was not so already, that as pagans we face a constant uphill battle to achieve such recognition.

For Cox, religion focuses on "non-falsifiable alternate realities that are postulated by and legitimated within identifiable communities through the transmission of an authoritative tradition" (Cox, 2007, pp.92-93). He goes on to add that through this, a religious community is able to collectively share in acts of remembrance of the past and these give meaning to the present. This definition can be applied to Shamanism, in the same way as it can be applied to the so-called "world religions". Consequently, it can be argued that it deserves the same kind of status.

Through active involvement in organisations such as the

British Association for the Study of Religions (BASR), the International Association for the History of Religions (IAHR), and Pagan Federation International (PFI), by attending and / or giving papers at Conferences, writing books and / or articles and, above all, by the way we conduct ourselves as representatives of what we believe in and practise, we can help to bring this about. For surely, all religions, in a comparative sense, deserve equal scholarly treatment, and it is up to us to make sure that they do. Hopefully, this book and those who read it will contribute towards the process.

The Pagan Federation **www.paganfed.org** was founded in 1971 to provide information on Paganism and to counter misconceptions about the religion. It works for the rights of Pagans (defined as followers of polytheistic or pantheistic nature-worshipping religions) to worship freely and without censure, as they are entitled to under Article 18 of the Universal Declaration of Human Rights. It publishes a quarterly journal, *Pagan Dawn*, arranges members-only and public events, and maintains personal contact by letter with individual members and with the wider Pagan community. Additionally, Conferences and regional gatherings are held throughout the UK and in other countries too. As for the British Association for the Study of Religions **www.basr.ac.uk**, it is affiliated to the International Association for the History of Religions (IAHR), whose object is the promotion of the academic study of religions through the international collaboration of all scholars whose research has a bearing on the subject. The BASR pursues these aims within the United Kingdom through the arrangement of conferences and symposia, the publication of a Bulletin and an Annual General Meeting. Membership of the BASR is open to scholars whose work has a bearing on the academic study of religions and who are normally resident in the United Kingdom.

***

As the title suggests, the book is primarily a collection of shamanic journeys and shamanic stories. Wherever people meet, stories are told and they have been told since time immemorial. The storytellers themselves have been described as the bridge to other times and ancient teachings and the telling of the stories helps to keep these teachings alive.

The earliest stories were probably chants or songs of praise for the natural world in pagan times. Later, dance and music accompanied stories. The storyteller would become the entertainer for the community and the historian, musician and poet too. The tales that were passed on from one generation to the next by word of mouth included epics, myths, parables, fables, fairy tales, folk tales, and shamanic stories too.The art of storytelling was particularly popular in England from around AD400 to 1500. Storytellers would travel around visiting markets, villages, towns and royal courts. They gathered news, swapped stories and learned regional tales in the process. When popular tales began to be printed cheaply in pamphlets known as chapbooks and sold by peddlers, the popularity of storytellers started to wane. With the advent of the mass media, the storyteller has unfortunately become more or less extinct. Attempts are being made to revive the art of storytelling and the profession of the storyteller, but unfortunately with only limited success.

A shamanic journey is one that generally takes place in a trance state to the sound of a drumbeat, through dancing, or by ingesting psychoactive drugs, in which aid is sought from beings in (what are considered to be) other realities generally for healing purposes or for divination—both for individuals and / or the community. A shamanic story can be defined as one that has either been based on or inspired by a shamanic journey, or one that contains a number of the elements typical of such a journey.

There is also a chapter devoted to Mircea Eliade, the historian of religions, whose seminal work, *Shamanism: Archaic Techniques of Esctasy*, originally published in French in 1951, led to the

3

revival of interest in the subject, to Carlos Castaneda's *Don Juan* books, and to the anthropologist Michael Harner setting up The Foundation for Shamanic Studies.

***

Note: The quotes are taken from Cox, J.L. (2007) *From Primitive to Indigenous*, Aldershot, Hampshire: Ashgate Publishing Limited.

Shamanism and the Language of the Animals

`In a strange region he scales steep slopes
Far from his friends he cuts a lonely figure...
So momentous are his travels among the mountains
To tell just a tenth would be a tall order

These lines from *Sir Gawain and the Green Knight* could also be used to describe the way of the shaman, because he/she lives a life apart from other too, and has difficulty in conveying in words just what it is that he/she experiences when journeying into other realities. Shamans have their own ways of describing trance experience. Outsiders

might call them 'metaphors', but to shamans these metaphors, such as 'death', are real, lived experiences ... 'Metaphor is a problematic term extracted from Western literary discourse which does not do justice to non-Western, non-literary shamanic experiences. In recognising this limitation, 'metaphor may remain a useful term for explaining alien shamanic experiences in terms understandable to Westerners (Wallis, 2003, p.116).

Perhaps this is why the accounts of memorable shamanic journeys were often turned into folktales, as it was the only way to make them both understandable and acceptable to people not familiar with the landscapes to be found and experiences to be had in such worlds. It is such tales, and the inner journeys these can take us on, that form the basis of this book.

So what is Shamanism? We could simply say that what shamans practise, whether they call themselves indigenous,

5

urban or neo-shamans, is what shamanism is, but this would just be avoiding the question and would be of little help to anyone. Instead, the following definition is proposed:

A shaman is understood to be someone who performs an ecstatic (in a trance state), imitative, or demonstrative ritual of a séance (or a combination of all three), at will (in other words, whenever he or she chooses to do so), in which aid is sought from beings in (what are considered to be) other realities generally for healing purposes or for divination–both for individuals and / or the community.

As for the practice of Shamanism, it is understood to encompass a personalistic view of the world, in which life is seen to be not only about beliefs and practices, but also about relation-ships–how we are related, and how we relate to each other. In Shamanism the notion of interdependence "is the idea of the kinship of all life, the recognition that nothing can exist in and of itself without being in relationship to other things, and therefore that it is insane for us to consider ourselves as essentially unrelated parts of the whole Earth" (Halifax in Nicholson, (comp.), 1987, p.220). And through neurotheology, this assertion so often heard expressed in neo-shamanic circles that all life is connected, can now be substantiated. This is because

it has been shown that during mystical ecstasy (or its equiv-alent, entheogenic shamanic states [states induced by ingesting hallucinogens]), the individual experiences a blurring of the boundaries on the ego and feels at "one with Nature"; the ego is no longer confined within the body, but extends outward to all of Nature; other living beings come to share in the ego, as an authentic communion with the total environment, which is sensed as in some way divine (Ruck, Staples, et al., 2007, p.76).

The use of the uncountable noun Shamanism, as opposed to the use of the plural form of the countable noun that is favoured by a number of writers on the subject, can be supported because other world religions, which are equally diverse, are also approached under a general heading. Also because the sense of extreme diversity among different forms of Shamanism has been exaggerated by the methods of anthropological research and in fact there are only a limited number of elements to be found running through its different forms, which can be organised usefully into categories for comparative purposes.

However, by assuming each has characteristics in common with the other, it can be argued that the study of indigenous peoples is being approached under hidden essentialist assumptions (see Cox, 2007, p.53). This is why it is important not to ignore the global interpenetration of religious movements when looking at any one form of shamanism. We find, for example, in some regions of the Caucasus paganism has been interpenetrated by Islam, in other regions by Orthodox Christianity, and in some cases both. Another point that needs to be made is that indigenous is used here to refer to people who identify themselves as belonging to, though not necessarily living in, a certain place, and thus includes diasporas.

In the story that will be presented in this chapter, the way in which the hero understands the language of the birds and is able to communicate with them marks him out as having special abilities and being different from others, as someone suitable to receive the "call" to become a future shaman for his community. And as is typical in shamanic stories, it is through the hero's ability to understand the language of the animals that he achieves the outcome he desires.

The shamanic story can be defined as one that has either been based on or inspired by a shamanic journey, or one that contains a number of the elements typical of such a journey, and the story presented here is just one of many such examples that can be

7

found. Brother Grimm's fairy tale *The Three Languages* is all about learning the language of the animals too, and then showing how it comes in useful–the way the two white doves teach the new Pope to say Mass, for example.

The religious beliefs within community religions of oral societies are characterized by a strong pragmatic element aimed at securing health and well being for the community, usual through ritual activity. This requires specialists, such as shamans, who can receive communication from the spirits, interpret the cause of any misfortune, and prescribe a 'cure' for it (see Platvoet, 1992, p.24). On the other hand, among those trained in Core Shamanism by practitioners such as Michael Harner and Jonathan Horwitz, there is not always a community available for them to be members of. That is why their focus tends to more on securing the health and well being of those individuals who consult them as clients.

Not only was the ability to understand the language of animals a traditional attribute of indigenous shamans, but so was the ability to shape-shift from human into animal shape. Sometimes this change is a literal one, human flesh transformed into animal flesh or covered over by animal skin; in other accounts, the soul leaves the shaman's unconscious body to enter into the body of an animal, fish or bird. And it is not only shamans who have such powers according to tales from around the globe. Shape shifting is part of a mythic and story-telling tradition stretching back over thousands of years. The gods of various mythologies are credited with this ability, as are the heroes of the great epic sagas.

In Nordic myth, Odin could change his shape into any beast or bird; in Greek myth, Zeus often assumed animal shape in his relentless pursuit of young women. Cernunnos, the lord of animals in Celtic mythology, wore the shape of a stag, and also the shape of a man with a heavy rack of horns. In the Odyssey, Homer tells the tale of Proteus — a famous soothsayer who

8

would not give away his knowledge unless forced to do so. Menelaus came upon him while he slept, and held on to him tightly as he shape-shifted into a lion, a snake, a leopard, a bear, etc. Defeated, Proteus returned to his own shape and Menelaus won the answers to his questions.

Not all transformations are from human to animal shape. The Great Selkie of Sule Skerry described in Scottish ballads, is a man upon dry land, a selkie (seal) in the sea, and he leaves a human maid pregnant with his child. And Irish legends tell of men who marry seal or otter women and then hide their animal skins from them to prevent them from returning to the water. Generally these women bear several sons, but pine away for their true home. If they manage to find the skin, they then return to the sea with barely a thought for the ones left behind.

Shamanic cultures today still recognise animals as mentors and allies, who not only enable us to access pathways to power but can also provide the guidance and support we need for the greater human journeys we are called on to undertake Speaking with the animals is something that is innate, something that we have forgotten, but something that can be relearned. After all, we evolved from animals, and because of this we still hold, deeply buried within the subconscious, the memories of these powers that we once possessed. And now for the story:

The Language of the Birds

Somewhere in a town in holy Russia, there lived a rich merchant with his wife. He had an only son, a dear, bright, and brave boy called Ivan. One lovely day Ivan sat at the dinner table with his parents. Near the window in the same room hung a cage, and a nightingale, a sweet-voiced, grey bird, was imprisoned within. The sweet nightingale began to sing its wonderful song with trills and high silvery tones. The merchant listened and listened to the song and said:

"How I wish I could understand the meaning of the different

9

songs of all the birds! I would give half my wealth to the man, if only there were such a man, who could make plain to me all the different songs of the different birds."

Ivan took notice of these words and no matter where he went, no matter where he was, no matter what he did, he always thought of how he could learn the language of the birds.

Some time after this the merchant's son happened to be hunting in a forest. The winds rose, the sky became clouded, the lightning flashed, the thunder roared loudly, and the rain fell in torrents. Ivan soon came near a large tree and saw a big nest in the branches. Four small birds were in the nest; they were quite alone, and neither father nor mother was there to protect them from the cold and wet. The good Ivan pitied them, climbed the tree and covered the little ones with his "kaftan," a long-skirted coat which the Russian peasants and merchants usually wear. The thunderstorm passed by and a big bird came flying and sat down on a branch near the nest and spoke very kindly to Ivan.

"Ivan, I thank thee; thou hast protected my little children from the cold and rain and I wish to do something for thee. Tell me what thou dost wish."

Ivan answered; "I am not in need; I have everything for my comfort. But teach me the birds' language."

"Stay with me three days and thou shalt know all about it."

Ivan remained in the forest three days. He understood well the teaching of the big bird and returned home more clever than before. One beautiful day soon after this Ivan sat with his parents when the nightingale was singing in his cage. His song was so sad, however, so very sad, that the merchant and his wife also became sad, and their son, their good Ivan, who listened very attentively, was even more affected, and the tears came running down his cheeks.

"What is the matter?" asked his parents; "what art thou weeping about, dear son?"

"Dear parents," answered the son, "it is because I understand the meaning of the nightingale's song, and because this meaning is so sad for all of us."

"What then is the meaning? Tell us the whole truth; do not hide it from us," said the father and mother.

"Oh, how sad it sounds!" replied the son. "How much better would it be never to have been born!"

"Do not frighten us," said the parents, alarmed. "If thou dost really understand the meaning of the song, tell us at once."

"Do you not hear for yourselves? The nightingale says: 'The time will come when Ivan, the merchant's son, shall become Ivan, the king's son, and his own father shall serve him as a simple servant.'"

The merchant and his wife felt troubled and began to distrust their son, their good Ivan. So one night they gave him a drowsy drink, and when he had fallen asleep they took him to a boat on the wide sea, spread the white sails, and pushed the boat from the shore.

For a long time the boat danced on the waves and finally it came near a large merchant vessel, which struck against it with such a shock that Ivan awoke. The crew on the large vessel saw Ivan ·and pitied him. So they decided to take him along with them and did so. High, very high, above in the sky they perceived cranes. Ivan said to the sailors: "Be careful; I hear the birds predicting a storm. Let us enter a harbour or we shall suffer great danger and damage. All the sails will be torn and all the masts will be broken."

But no one paid any attention and they went farther on. In a short time the storm arose, the wind tore the vessel almost to pieces, and they had a very hard time to repair all the damage. When they were through with their work they heard many wild swans flying above them and talking very loud among themselves.

"What are they talking about?" inquired the men, this time with interest.

"Be careful," advised Ivan. "I hear and distinctly understand them to say that the pirates, the terrible sea robbers, are near. If we do not enter a harbour at once they will imprison and kill us."

The crew quickly obeyed this advice and as soon as the vessel entered the harbour the pirate boats passed by and the merchants saw them capture several unprepared vessels. When the danger was over, the sailors with Ivan went farther, still farther. Finally the vessel anchored near a town, large and unknown to the merchants. A king ruled in that town who was very much annoyed by three black crows. These three crows were all the time perching near the window of the king's chamber. No one knew how to get rid of them and no one could kill them. The king ordered notices to be placed at all crossings and on all prominent buildings, saying that whoever was able to relieve the king from the noisy birds would be rewarded by obtaining the youngest korolevna [princess], the king's daughter, for a wife; but the one who should have the daring to undertake but not succeed in delivering the palace from the crows would have his head cut off. Ivan attentively read the announcement, once, twice, and once more. Finally he made the sign of the cross and went to the palace. He said to the servants:

"Open the window and let me listen to the birds."

The servants obeyed and Ivan listened for a while. Then he said:

"Show me to your sovereign king."

When he reached the room where the king sat on a high, rich chair, he bowed and said:

"There are three crows, a father crow, a mother crow, and a son crow. The trouble is that they desire to obtain thy royal decision as to whether the son crow must follow his father crow or his mother crow."

The king answered: "The son crow must follow the father crow."

As soon as the king announced his royal decision the crow

father with the crow son went one way and the crow mother disappeared the other way, and no one has heard the noisy birds since. The king gave one-half of his kingdom and his youngest korolevna to Ivan, and a happy life began for him.

In the meantime his father, the rich merchant, lost his wife and by and by his fortune also. There was no one left to take care of him, and the old man went begging under the windows of charitable people. He went from one window to another, from one village to another, from one town to another, and one bright day he came to the palace where Ivan lived, begging humbly for charity. Ivan saw him and recognized him, ordered him to come inside, and gave him food to eat and also supplied him with good clothes, asking questions:

"Dear old man, what can I do for thee?" he said.

"If thou art so very good," answered the poor father, without knowing that he was speaking to his own son, "let me remain here and serve thee among thy faithful servants."

"Dear, dear father!" exclaimed Ivan, "thou didst doubt the true song of the nightingale, and now thou seest that our fate was to meet according to the predictions of long ago."

The old man was frightened and knelt before his son, but his Ivan remained the same good son as before, took his father lovingly into his arms, and together they wept over their sorrow.

Several days passed by and the old father felt courage to ask his son, the korolevitch:

"Tell me, my son, how was it that thou didst not perish in the boat?"

Ivan Korolevitch laughed gaily.

"I presume," he answered, "that it was not my fate to perish at the bottom of the wide sea, but my fate was to marry the korolevna, my beautiful wife, and to sweeten the old age of my dear father."

Note: The story is taken from *Folk Tales from the Russian* retold by Verra Xenophontovna Kalamatiano de Blumenthal [1903] Scanned, proofed and formatted at sacred-texts.com by John Bruno Hare, March 2002. This text is in the public domain in the US because it was published prior to 1923.

References

Berman, M. (2009) *Shamanic Journeys through the Caucasus*, Hampshire: O-Books.

Berman, M. (2010) *Guided Visualisations through the Caucasus*, California: Pendraig Publishing.

Cox, J.L. (2007) *From Primitive to Indigenous*, Aldershot, Hampshire: Ashgate Publishing Limited.

Halifax, J. (1987) "Shamanism, Mind, and No Self" in Nicholson, S. (comp.) *Shamanism: An Expanded View of Reality*, Wheaton: The Theosophical Publishing House.

Platvoet J.G. (1992) 'African Traditional Religions in the Religious History of Humankind', in *Religious Education. A Resource Book with Special Reference to Zimbabwe*. Utrecht: Utrecht University, 11-28. Reprinted 1993, *Journal for the Study Of Religion* 6 (2): 29-48.

Ruck, Carl A.P., Staples, B.D., Celdran J.A.G., Hoffman, M.A. (2007) *The Hidden World: Survival of Pagan Shamanic Themes in European Fairytales*, North Carolina: Carolina Academic Press.

Wallis, Robert J. (2003) *Shamans/Neo-Shamans: Ecstasy, Alternative Archaeologies and Contemporary Pagans*, London: Routledge.

A Journey to the Land of the Dead

Although the cosmology of the world of the shaman will vary from culture to culture, the structure of the whole cosmos is frequently symbolized by the number seven, and is made up of the four directions, the centre, the zenith in heaven, and the nadir in the underworld. The essential axes of this structure are the four cardinal points and a central vertical axis passing through their point of intersection that connects the Upper World, the Middle World and the Lower World. The names by which the central vertical axis that connects the three worlds is referred to include the world pole, the tree of life, the sacred mountain, the central house pole, and Jacob's ladder. So important is this cosmology considered to be that religion itself has been described by Berger (1969) as the enterprise we undertake to establish just such a sacred cosmos.

Different types of shamanic journeys can be undertaken–to the Lower World where you can make contact with Power Animals and to the Upper World where you can meet your Sacred Teacher. "While it is true that man depends on his gods, the dependence is mutual. The gods also need man, without offerings and sacrifices, they would die" (Durkheim, 2001, p.38). This applies equally well to the Sacred Teachers and Power Animals met by shamanic practitioners on their journeys to other realities. This is why the shaman is required to both respect and honour these Helpers who assist him or else they will desert him.

Dr Knud Rasmussen, who was born and raised among the Greenland Eskimos, recorded an account of an Iglulik shaman's Lower World journey to the Sea Spirit Takanakapsaluk. When the Sea Spirit gets angry at men's failings to live as they should, she is said to call up storms to prevent them from hunting, to steal souls and to send sickness among the people. The shaman is then called upon to journey to the bottom of the sea where she lives. He does so either on behalf of individuals seeking help or on behalf of the whole community to mediate with her. Dangers on the journey include three large rolling stones he is required to pass between, and a snarling dog that guards the entrance to her house. There he smoothes and combs her tangled and matted hair to placate her. On his return, all those present at the séance are required to confess to any taboos they have broken, which are believed to be the cause of the ills brought upon them by the Sea Spirit. For a complete account of the journey, well worth reading, see Rasmussen (1929).

The starting point for a journey to the Upper World can be a mountain, a treetop, or even a ladder, from which the shaman envisions himself ascending into the sky; "and despite the variety of socio-religious contexts in which it occurs, the ascent always has the same goal–meeting with the Gods or heavenly powers, in order to obtain a blessing (whether a personal consecration, a favour for the community, or the cure of a sick person)" (Eliade, 1958, p.77). At some stage of the journey the shaman may come up against a kind of barrier that temporarily impedes the ascent. But once this has been successfully negotiated, the Upper World is reached. As everyone's experience of the process is unique, generalizing about it is not particularly helpful. However, to give some idea of what it can be like, there follows a brief personal account.

My own means of accessing the Upper World, which I do to the sound of a drum, either played for me or on cassette and listened to through headphones, is by "journeying" back to the garden of the house I grew up in and climbing the trunk of a tree there. When I climb high enough to pass into what I call "the blue zone" where the atmosphere clings to me and makes me feel heavy, I walk along a branch that runs at right angles to the trunk, then jump down on to a spongy mound of grass to find myself under the leaves of what appears to be a Willow tree. There I follow a path that runs along the side of a fast-flowing river, passing through heath land, until I come to the gravel pathway that leads to the house where my Sacred Teacher lives. There I lift the iron knocker and strike the door three times. It is opened by the diminutive doorkeeper, always immaculately turned out, in a smart double-breasted blue blazer and white slacks with perfect creases, not a hair out of place. I greet him courteously, and then walk down the corridor with the bare floorboards that creak underfoot until I come to the door at the end. I turn the round wooden handle and open it to find my Sacred Teacher waiting for me. I go there when I have philosophical questions I need answers to, rather than to look for the support of my Power Animals which I find in the Lower World.

Journeys are also undertaken to the Land of the Dead, where the shaman acts as a psychopomp–a conductor of souls. Sometimes the Land of the Dead is antipodal, meaning every-thing there is reversed: day here is night there, and vice versa. And it is not always necessary to be dead in order to visit ghost land. In eastern Melanesia, living people can go down to the netherworld, Panoi, either in the body or in spirit, and either in dream or in a near-death state. Ghosts advise them not to eat from the food of the dead, for otherwise they cannot come back alive (Couliano, 1991, p.37).

There are also journeys for the purpose of divination and journeys to carry out Soul Retrievals. Soul loss is the term used to describe the way parts of the psyche become detached when we are faced with traumatic situations. In psychological terms, it is known as dissociation and it works as a defence mechanism, a means of displacing unpleasant feelings, impulses or thoughts into the unconscious. In shamanic terms, these split off parts can be found in non-ordinary reality and are only accessible to those familiar with its topography (see Gagan, 1998, p.9).

As for Middle-world journeys, accounts of these have been recorded in areas where food supplies are precarious and migrating animal herds must be located such as in the near-

Arctic areas of North America and Siberia. Such journeys are undertaken to see events that take place in this reality in their non-ordinary reality forms and to gain a greater insight into their nature. But what is this other dimension of our world like and how can it be described to someone who has never experienced it? For each person who "journeys" the experience is unique so generalisation cannot be particularly accurate. However, this is what Sandra Ingerman, the neo-shamanic practitioner, has to say about it:

> In non-ordinary reality, the Middle World comes closest to our ordinary reality. Here I see scenes that I would experience in my waking life, but I am in an altered state of consciousness when looking at them. ... Shamans usually travel to the Middle World to find lost and stolen objects. I also travel to the Middle World to speak to the spirit of a client who is in a coma or unconscious to get permission to do healing work on his or her behalf (Ingerman, 1993, p.172).

How can these other worlds be accessed? The journey frequently involves passing through some kind of gateway. As Eliade explains,

> [The] "clashing of rocks," the "dancing reeds," the gates in the shape of jaws, the "two razor-edged restless mountains," the "two clashing icebergs," the "active door," the "revolving barrier," the door made of the two halves of the eagle's beak, and many more – all these are images used in myths and sagas to suggest the insurmountable difficulties of passage to the Other World (Eliade, 2003, pp.64-65).

And to make such a journey requires a change in one's mode of being, entering a transcendent state, which makes it possible to attain the world of spirit. The journey undertaken in the Native

American tale that follows, taken from Andrew Lang's *The Yellow Fairy Book*, is one to the Land of the Dead.

In the Land of Souls

Far away, in North America, where the Red Indians dwell, there lived a long time ago a beautiful maiden, who was lovelier than any other girl in the whole tribe. Many of the young braves sought her in marriage, but she would listen to one only—a handsome chief, who had taken her fancy some years before. So they were to be married, and great rejoicings were made, and the two looked forward to a long life of happiness together, when the very night before the wedding feast a sudden illness seized the girl, and, without a word to her friends who were weeping round her, she passed silently away.

The heart of her lover had been set upon her, and the thought of her remained with him night and day. He put aside his bow, and went neither to fight nor to hunt, but from sunrise to sunset he sat by the place where she was laid, thinking of his happiness that was buried there. At last, after many days, a light seemed to come to him out of the darkness. He remembered having heard from the old, old people of the tribe, that there was a path that led to the Land of Souls—that if you sought carefully you could find it.

So the next morning he got up early, and put some food in his pouch and slung an extra skin over his shoulders, for he knew not how long his journey would take, nor what sort of country he would have to go through. Only one thing he knew, that if the path was there, he would find it. At first he was puzzled, as there seemed no reason he should go in one direction more than another. Then all at once he thought he had heard one of the old men say that the Land of Souls lay to the south, and so, filled with new hope and courage, he set his face southwards. For many, many miles the country looked the same as it did round his own home. The forests, the hills, and the rivers all seemed exactly like the ones he had left. The only thing that was different was the snow, which had lain thick upon the hills and trees when he started, but grew less and less the farther he went south, till it disappeared altogether. Soon the trees put forth their buds, and flowers sprang up under his feet, and instead of thick clouds there was blue sky over his head, and everywhere the birds were singing. Then he knew that he was in the right road.

The thought that he should soon behold his lost bride made his heart beat for joy, and he sped along lightly and swiftly. Now his way led through a dark wood, and then over some steep cliffs, and on the top of these he found a hut or wigwam. An old man clothed in skins, and holding a staff in his hand, stood in the doorway; and he said to the young chief who was beginning to tell his story, 'I was waiting for you, wherefore you have come I know. It is but a short while since she whom you seek was here. Rest in my hut, as she also rested, and I will tell you what you ask, and whither you should go.'

On hearing these words, the young man entered the hut, but his heart was too eager within him to suffer him to rest, and when he arose, the old man rose too, and stood with him at the door. 'Look,' he said, 'at the water which lies far out yonder, and the plains which stretch beyond. That is the Land of Souls, but no man enters it without leaving his body behind him. So, lay down your body here; your bow and arrows, your skin and your dog. They shall be kept for you safely.'

Then he turned away, and the young chief, light as air, seemed hardly to touch the ground; and as he flew along the scents grew sweeter and the flowers more beautiful, while the animals rubbed their noses against him, instead of hiding as he approached, and birds circled round him, and fishes lifted up their heads and looked as he went by. Very soon he noticed with wonder, that neither rocks nor trees barred his path. He passed through them without knowing it, for indeed, they were not rocks and trees at all, but only the souls of them; for this was the

Land of Shadows.

So he went on with winged feet till he came to the shores of a great lake, with a lovely island in the middle of it; while on the bank of the lake was a canoe of glittering stone, and in the canoe were two shining paddles.

The chief jumped straight into the canoe, and seizing the paddles pushed off from the shore, when to his joy and wonder he saw following him in another canoe exactly like his own the maiden for whose sake he had made this long journey. But they could not touch each other, for between them rolled great waves, which looked as if they would sink the boats, yet never did. And the young man and the maiden shrank with fear, for down in the depths of the water they saw the bones of those who had died before, and in the waves themselves men and women were struggling, and but few passed over. Only the children had no fear, and reached the other side in safety. Still, though the chief and the young girl quailed in terror at these horrible sights and sounds, no harm came to them, for their lives had been free from evil, and the Master of Life had said that no evil should happen unto them. So they reached unhurt the shore of the Happy Island, and wandered through the flowery fields and by the banks of rushing streams, and they knew not hunger nor thirst; neither cold nor heat. The air fed them and the sun warmed them, and they forgot the dead, for they saw no graves, and the young man's thoughts turned not to wars, neither to the hunting of animals. And gladly would these two have walked thus for ever, but in the murmur of the wind he heard the Master of Life saying to him, 'Return whither you came, for I have work for you to do, and your people need you, and for many years you shall rule over them. At the gate my messenger awaits you, and you shall take again your body which you left behind, and he will show you what you are to do. Listen to him, and have patience, and in time to come you shall rejoin her whom you must now leave, for she is accepted, and will remain ever young and

21

beautiful, as when I called her hence from the Land of Snows.'

References

Berger, P. (1973) *The Social Reality of Religion*, Harmondsworth: Penguin

Berman, M. (2007) *The Nature of Shamanism and the Shamanic Story*, Newcastle: Cambridge Scholars Publishing.

Couliano, I.P. (1991) *Out of this World*, Boston: Shambhala.

Durkheim, E. (2001) *The Elementary Forms of Religious Life*, Oxford: Oxford University Press (originally published in 1912).

Eliade, M. (2003) *Rites and Symbols of Initiation*, Putnam, Connecticut: Spring Publications (originally published by Harper Bros., New York, 1958).

Gagan, J.M. (1998) *Journeying: where shamanism and psychology meet*, Santa Fe, NM: Rio Chama Pubications.

Lang A. (ed.) (1894) *The Yellow Fairy Book*, London, New York: Longmans, Green, and Co.

Rasmussen, K. (1929) *Intellectual Culture of the Iglulik Eskimos*, from vol. VII of Report of the Fifth Thule Expedition, 1921-24, Copenhagen: Gyldendalske Boghandel, Nordisk Forlag.

The Water of Life of Ka-ne:
A Legend of Old Hawaii

"When the moon dies she goes to the living water of Ka-ne, to the water which can restore everything to life, even the moon to the path in the sky." —*Maori Legend of New Zealand.*

The Waters have been described as the reservoir of all the potentialities of existence because they not only precede every form but they also serve to sustain every creation. Immersion is equivalent to dissolution of form, in other words death, whereas emergence repeats the cosmogonic act of formal manifestation, in other words re-birth (see Eliade, 1952, p.151).

The idea of regeneration through water can be found in numerous pan-cultural tales about the miraculous Fountain of Youth, and water can be seen to be both purifying and regenerative. So pervasive were these legends that in the 16th century the Spanish conquistador Ponce de Leon actually set out to find it once and for all — and found Florida instead.

The Hawaiians of long ago shared in the belief that somewhere along the deep sea beyond the horizon around their islands, or somewhere in the cloud-land above the heavens which rested on their mountains, there was a place known as "The land of the water of life of the gods." And in this land was a lake of living water which held the power to restore everything to life. This water was called in the Hawaiian language Ka wai ola a Ka-ne, literally "The water living of Ka-ne," or "The water of life of Ka-ne." Mention of this "wai ola" is found in the folklore of many of the Pacific island groups, such as New Zealand, the Tongas, Samoa, Tahiti and the Hawaiian Islands.

Ka-ne was one of the four greatest gods of the Polynesians, and in his hands was placed the care of the water of life. If any person secured this water, the power of the god went with it. A sick person drinking it would recover health, and a dead person sprinkled with it would be restored to life.

***

In the misty past of the Hawaiian Islands a king was very, very ill. All his friends thought that he was going to die. The family came together in the enclosure around the house where the sick man lay. Three sons were wailing sorely because of their heavy grief.

An old man, a stranger passing by, asked them the cause of the trouble. One of the young men replied, "Our father lies in that house very near death."

The old man looked over the wall upon the young men and said slowly: "I have heard of something which would make your father well. He must drink of the water of life of Ka-ne. But this is very hard to find and difficult to get."

The old man disappeared, but the eldest son said, "I shall not fail to find this water of life, and I shall be my father's favourite and shall have the kingdom." He ran to his father for permission to go and find this water of life.

The old king said: "No, there are many difficulties and even death in the way. It is better to die here." The young prince urged his father to let him try, and at last received permission.

The prince, taking his water calabash, hastened away. As he went along a path through the forest, suddenly an ugly little man, a dwarf (an a-a), appeared in his path and called out, "Where are you going that you are in such a hurry?" The prince answered roughly: "Is this your business? I have nothing to say to you." He pushed the little man aside and ran on.

The dwarf was very angry and determined to punish the rough speaker, so he made the path twist and turn and grow narrow before the traveller. The further the prince ran, the more

24

bewildered he was, and the more narrow became the way, and thicker and thicker were the trees and vines and ferns through which the path wound. At last he fell to the earth, crawling and fighting against the tangled masses of ferns and the clinging tendrils of the vines of the land of fairies and gnomes. They twined themselves around him and tied him tight with living coils, and finally he lay like one who was dead.

For a long time the family waited and at last came to the conclusion that he had been overcome by some difficulty. The second son said that he would go and find that water of life, so taking his water calabash he ran swiftly along the path which his brother had taken. His thought was also the selfish one, that he might succeed where his brother had failed and so win the kingdom.

As he ran along he met the same little man, who was the king of the fairies although he appeared as a dwarf. The little man called out, "Where are you going in such a hurry?"

The prince spoke roughly, pushed him out of the way, and rushed on. Soon he also was caught in the tangled woods and held fast like one who was dead.

Then the last, the youngest son, took his calabash and went away thinking that he might be able to rescue his brothers as well as get the water of life for his father. He met the same little man, who asked him where he was going. He told the dwarf about the king's illness and the report of the "water of life of Ka-ne," and asked the dwarf if he could aid in any way. "For," said the prince, "my father is near death, and this living water will heal him and I do not know the way."

The little man said: "Because you have spoken gently and have asked my help and have not been rough and rude as were your brothers, I will tell you where to go and will give you aid. The path will open before you at the bidding of this strong staff which I give you. By and by you will come to the palace of a king who is a sorcerer. In his house is the fountain of that water of life.

25

You cannot get into that house unless you take three bundles of food which I will give you. Take the food in one hand and your strong staff in the other. Strike the door of that king's house three times with your staff and an opening will be made. Then you will see two dragons with open mouths ready to devour you. Quickly throw food in their mouths and they will become quiet. Fill your calabash with the living water and hurry away. At midnight the doors will be shut, and you cannot escape."

The prince thanked the little man, took the presents and went his way rejoicing, and after a long time he came to the strange land and the sorcerer's house. Three times he struck until he broke the wall and made a door for himself. He saw the dragons and threw the food into their mouths, making them his friends. He went in and saw some young chiefs, who welcomed him and gave him a war-club and a bundle of food. He went on to another room, where he met a beautiful maiden whom he loved at once with all his heart. She told him as she looked in his eyes that after a time they would meet again and live as husband and wife. Then she showed him where he could get the water of life, and warned him to be in haste. He dipped his calabash in the spring and leaped through the door just at the stroke of midnight.

With great joy he hastened from land to land and from sea to sea watching for the little man, the a-a, who had aided him so much. As if his wish were known soon the little man appeared and asked him how he fared on his journey. The prince told him about the long way and his success and then offered to pay as best he could for all the aid so kindly given.

The dwarf refused all reward. Then the prince said he would be so bold as to ask one favour more. The little man said, "You have been so thoughtful in dealing with me as one highly honoured by you, ask and perhaps I can give you what you wish."

The prince said, "I do not want to return home without my brothers; can you help me find them?" "They are dead in the forest," said the dwarf. "If you find them they will only do you harm. Let them rest in their beds of vines and ferns. They have evil hearts."

But the young chief pressed his kindly thought and the dwarf showed him the tangled path through the forest. With his magic staff he opened the way and found his brothers. He sprinkled a little of the water of life over them and strength returned to them. He told them how he had found the "living water of Ka-ne," and had received gifts and also the promise of a beautiful bride. The brothers forgot their long death-like sleep and were jealous and angry at the success of their younger brother.

They journeyed far before they reached home. They passed a strange land where the high chief was resisting a large body of rebels. The land was lying desolate and the people were starving. The young prince pitied the high chief and his people and gave them a part of the bundle of food from the house of the god Ka-ne. They ate and became very strong. Then he let the chief have his war-club. Quickly the rebels were destroyed and the land had quiet and peace.

He aided another chief in his wars, and still another in his difficulties, and at last came with his brothers to the seacoast of his own land. There they lay down to sleep, but the wicked brothers felt that there were no more troubles in which they would need the magic aid of their brother, so they first planned to kill him, but the magic war-club seemed to defend him. Then they took his calabash of the water of life and poured the water into their water-jars, filling his calabash again with salt, sickish sea-water. They went on home the next morning. The young prince pressed forward with his calabash, gave it to his father, telling him to drink and recover life. The king drank deeply of the salt water and was made more seriously sick, almost to death. Then the older brothers came, charging the young prince with an attempt to poison his father. They gave him the real water of life and he immediately became strong as in the days of his youth.

The king was very angry with the youngest son and sent him away with an officer who was skilled in the forest. The officer was a friend of the young prince and helped him to find a safe hiding-place, where he lived a long time.

By and by the three great kings came from distant lands with many presents for the prince who had given them peace and great prosperity. They told the father what a wonderful son he had, and wanted to give him their thanks. The father called the officer whom he had sent away with the young man and acknowledged the wrong he had done. The officer told him the prince was not dead, so the king sent messengers to find him.

Meanwhile one of the most beautiful princesses of all the world had sent word everywhere that she would be seated in her house and any prince who could walk straight to her along a line drawn in the air by her sorcerers, without turning to either side, should be her husband. There was a day set for the contest.

The messengers sent out by the king to find the prince knew all about this contest, so they made all things known to their young chief when they found him. He went with his swift steps of love to the land of the beautiful girl. His brothers had both failed in their most careful endeavours, but the young prince followed his heart's desire and went straight to a door which opened of its own accord. Out leaped the maiden of the palace of the land of Ka-ne. In to his arms she rushed and sent her servants everywhere to proclaim that her lord had been found.

The brothers ran away to distant lands and never returned. The prince and the princess became king and queen and lived in great peace and happiness, administering the affairs of their kingdom for the welfare of their subjects.

Westervelt, W.D. (1915) *Hawaiian Legends of Old Honolulu*, Boston, G.H. Ellis Press.

***

As Emily Lyle (2007) points out in the abstract to her paper "Narrative Form and the Structure of Myth", "At each stage in transmission of a tale from generation to generation, modifications take place but something remains. Thus there is a potential for material to be retained from a time in the distant past when the narrative was embedded in a total oral worldview or cosmology." In view of the fact that in the past shamanism was widely practised in the region where the tale presented here originates from, it should therefore come as no surprise that a shamanic worldview and shamanic cosmology is to be found embedded in it.

Stories have traditionally been classified as epics, myths, sagas, legends, folk tales, fairy tales, parables or fables. However, the definitions of the terms have a tendency to overlap (see Berman, 2006, p.150-152) making it difficult to classify and categorize material. Another problem with the traditional terminology is that the genre system formed on the basis of European folklore cannot be fully applied universally.

Consider, for example, Eliade's definition of myth. For Eliade the characteristics of myth, as experienced by archaic societies, are that it constitutes the absolutely true and sacred History of the acts of the Supernaturals, which is always related to a "creation", which leads to a knowledge, experienced ritually, of the origin of things and thus the ability to control them, and which is "lived" in the sense that one is profoundly affected by the power of the events it recreates (see Eliade, 1964, pp.18-19). However, many stories are "lived" in the sense that one is profoundly affected by the events they recreate without them necessarily being myths. Moreover, many shamanic stories, including neo-shamanic accounts of journeys, could be regarded as having the above characteristics but would still not necessarily be classified as myths.

Another problem encountered is that a number of the definitions of what a myth is are so general in nature that they tend to be of little value. For example, the suggestion that a myth is "a story about something significant [that] ... can take place in the past ... or in the present, or in the future" (Segal, 2004, p.5) really does not help us at all as this could be applied to more or less every type of tale. For this reason a case was argued in Berman (2006) for the introduction of a new genre, termed the shamanic story. This can be defined as a story that has either been based on or inspired by a shamanic journey, or one that contains a number of the elements typical of such a journey. Like other genres, it has "its own style, goals, entelechy, rhetoric, developmental pattern, and characteristic roles" (Turner, 1985, p.187), and like other genres it can be seen to differ to a certain extent from culture to culture. It should perhaps be noted at this point, however, that there are both etic and emic ways of regarding narrative (see Turner, 1982, p.65) and the term "shamanic story" clearly presents an outside view. It should also be pointed out that what is being offered here is a polythetic definition of what the shamanic story is, in which a pool of characteristics can apply, but need not.

Characteristics typical of the genre include the way in which many of the stories contain embedded texts (often the account of the shamanic journey itself), how the number of actors is clearly limited as one would expect in subjective accounts of what can be regarded as inner journeys, and how the stories tend to be used for healing purposes.

In his Foreword to *Tales of the Sacred and the Supernatural*, Eliade admits to repeatedly taking up "the themes of *sortie du temps*, or temporal dislocation, and of the alteration or the trans-mutation of space" (Eliade, 1981, p.10), and these are themes that appear over and over again in shamanic stories too.

Additionally, given that through the use of narrative shamans are able to provide their patients "with a language, by means of which unexpressed, and otherwise inexpressible, psychic states can be expressed" (Lévi-Strauss, 1968, p.198), it follows that another feature of shamanic stories is they have the potential to provide the same too.

They are also frequently examples of what Jürgen Kremer, transpersonal psychologist and spiritual practitioner, called "tales of power" after one of Carlos Castaneda's novels. He defines such texts as 'conscious verbal constructions based on numinous experiences in non-ordinary reality, "which guide individuals and help them to integrate the spiritual, mythical, or archetypal aspects of their internal and external experience in unique, meaningful, and fulfilling ways" (Kremer, 1988, p.192). In other words, they can serve the purpose of helping us reconnect with our indigenous roots.

The style of storytelling most frequently employed in both shamanic stories and in fairy tales is that of magic realism, in which although "the point of departure is 'realistic' (recognizable events in chronological succession, everyday atmosphere, verisimilitude, characters with more or less predictable psychological reactions), ... soon strange discontinuities or gaps appear in the 'normal,' true-to-life texture of the narrative" (Calinescu, 1978, p.386). In other words, what happens is that our expectations based on our intuitive knowledge of physics are ultimately breached and knocked out. It is, in effect, very much the style of storytelling that we find in *The Water of Life of Ka-ne*.

When it comes to the interpretation of any folktale, however, we need to keep in mind that every written text is no less an act of creating a new reality than of describing a given one.Consequently, there is no way in which any conclusions that are drawn about the way in which the tale reflects the lives and practices of the people at the time it relates to can be regarded as hard facts. And for this reason, all we can do, in effect, is to make educated guesses about such matters. At the same time, however, it should also be pointed out that absence of evidence is not evidence of absence either.

The shamanic journey frequently involves passing through some kind of gateway. And to make such a journey requires a change in one's mode of being, entering a transcendent state, which makes it possible to attain the world of spirit. (Berman, 2007, p.48).

In the case of *The Water of Life of Ka-ne*, the gateway is represented by the path that twists and turns, where travellers have to crawl and fight against the tangled masses of ferns and the clinging tendrils of the vines of the land of fairies and gnomes. There is then the door of the king's palace that has to be passed through, which is achieved with the aid of a magical staff given to the seeker by a Spirit Helper he encounters along the way. The Spirit Helper is in fact the king of the fairies although he appears to the hero as a dwarf.

The ability to shape-shift is one of the attributes often credited to shamans, and it is not only shamans who have such powers according to tales from around the globe. Shape shifting is part of a mythic and story-telling tradition stretching back over thousands of years. In Nordic myth, Odin could change his shape into any beast or bird; in Greek myth, Zeus often assumed animal shape in his relentless pursuit of young women. Cernunnos, the lord of animals in Celtic mythology, wore the shape of a stag, and also the shape of a man with a heavy rack of horns.

The number three plays an important part in the story, with their being three brothers, three bundles of food, and the requirement to knock on the door of the king's palace three times too. Not only does the number three appear in many folktales, (three brothers or sisters, three tasks to accomplish, three encounters, three guesses, three little pigs, three bears), but it also has mystical and spiritual associations. In ancient Babylon the three primary gods were Anu, Bel (Baal), and Ea, representing Heaven, Earth, and the Abyss. Similarly, there were three aspects to the Egyptian sun god: Khepri (rising), Re (midday), and Atum (setting). And in Christianity there is the Trinity of God the Father, God the Son, and God the Holy Spirit.

The Pythagoreans believed that man is a full chord, or eight notes, and deity comes next. Three is the perfect trinity and represents perfect unity, twice three is the perfect dual, and three times three is the perfect plural, which explains why nine was considered to be a mystical number. Our tale certainly has a mystical element to it, and its connection to such symbolism clearly gives it greater significance. However, one of the problems when it comes to considering symbolism is symbolic meaning can be read into almost anything and there is often no way of checking the interpretation.

The tale ends with the prince and the princess becoming king and queen. As a result the balance of the community, which was upset by the former king's illness, is restored once more. Although these days the neo-shamanic practitioner often works primarily to serve the needs of individual clients, the role of the indigenous shaman was more to do with maintaining the equilibrium of the whole community, and this is what the youngest son can be seen to re-establish in this tale.

With a journey into non-ordinary reality, shape-shifting, a meeting with a spirit helper, a quest entailing various ordeals that can be regarded as a process of initiation for our hero to see whether he is worthy to eventually take on the role that his father had previously performed, what we have here is essentially a shamanic story rather than what at first sight might appear to be just a simple fairy tale, and the same can be shown to be the case with other tales from the region too.

References

Berman, M. (2006) 'The Nature of Shamanism and the Shamanic Journey', unpublished M.Phil Thesis, University of Wales, Lampeter.

Berman, M. (2007) *The Nature of Shamanism and the Shamanic*

Story, Newcastle: Cambridge Scholars Publishing.

Berman, M. (2008) *Divination and the Shamanic Story*, Newcastle: Cambridge Scholars Publishing.

Calinescu, M. (1978) 'The Disguises of Miracle: Notes on Mircea Eliade's Fiction.' In Bryan Rennie (ed.) (2006) *Mircea Eliade: A Critical Reader*, London: Equinox Publishing Ltd.

Eliade, M. (1964) *Myth and Reality*, London: George Allen & Unwin

Eliade, M. (1981) *Tales of the Sacred and the Supernatural*, Philadelphia: The Westminster Press.

Eliade, M. (1991) Images and Symbols, New Jersey: Princeton University Press (The original edition is copyright Librairie Gallimard 1952).

Eliade, M. (2003) *Rites and Symbols of Initiation*, Putnam, Connecticut: Spring Publications (originally published by Harper Bros., New York, 1958).

Kremer, J.W. (1988) 'Shamanic Tales as Ways of Personal Empowerment.' In Gary Doore (ed.) *Shaman's Path: Healing, Personal Growth and Empowerment*, Boston, Massachusetts: Shambhala Publications. Pp.189-199.

Lévi-Strauss, C. (1968) *Structural Anthropology*, Harmondsworth: Penguin.

Lyle, E. (2007) 'Narrative Form and the Structure of Myth' in *Folklore 33* 59.

Segal, R.A. (2004) *Myth: A Very Short Introduction*, Oxford: Oxford University Press.

Turner, V. (1982) *From Ritual to Theatre: The Human Seriousness of Play*, New York: PAJ Publications (A division of Performing Arts Journal, Inc.).

Turner, V. (1985) *On the Edge of the Bush: Anthropology as Experience.* Tucson, AZ: University of Arizona Press.

Westervelt, W.D. (1915) *Hawaiian Legends of Old Honolulu*, Boston, G.H. Ellis Press.

The Future through the Writing on your Forehead

Armenians even today believe that there is writing on a person's forehead which tells his or her future and that this future is pre-determined. The Writer, or Grog, who is responsible for recording this is believed by many to be the good angel who sits on the right shoulder of each of us, urging us to do good things and keeping accurate records of such doings. The bad angel, on the other hand, sits on the left shoulder and encourages us to do wrong. This writer, Tir, was believed to be the scribe of the supreme god, Aramazd (see Hoogasian-Villa, 1966, p.323).

The deity who had first place among the Armenian gods was known by a number of names, and also had his own temple:

Ahramazd, l'Ahura Mazda du Zend-Avesta, Oromazès, Ormouzd ou Ormizd des auteurs de l'Occident. Ahramazd, comme Dieu supreme, avait chez les Arméniens le nom de Père de tous les Dieux. Les épithètes qui l'accompagnaient constamment étaient celles de: grand et fort, créateur du ciel et de la terre, produisant l'abondance et la fertilité.

Son temple se trouvait dans la province de Bardzer-Haïg, district de Darankh, dans le fort d'Ani, lieu de sépultre des rois arménienes de la dynastie des Arsacides. (Émin, 1864, pp.10-11).

Ani was Armenia's medieval capital, but is now in the modern Turkish state of Kars right along the border between the two countries.

Ani first rose to prominence in the 5th century A.D., as a hilltop fortress belonging to the Armenian Kamsarakan

Dynasty. By the ninth century, the Kamsarakan possessions in Eastern Anatolia had merged with the Bagratid Dynasty, and in 956, King Ashot III moved the Armenian capital to Ani. Shortly thereafter, the Armenian Catholics moved here as well, establishing the city as the undisputed center of Armenia. The city grew rapidly, and by the eleventh century, the city boasted more than 100,000 citizens. At its height of power and wealth, it became known as the *City of Forty Gates* and the *City of a Thousand* Churches (**http://wikitravel.org/en/Ani** [accessed 2/12/09]).

Those days have long since past, though, and all that remains is uninhabitable ruins.

Aramazd was regarded as the father of all gods and goddesses, the creator of heaven and earth. The first two letters in his name, "AR" is the Indo-European root for sun, light, and life, and Aramazd was the source of earth's fertility. Meeting with Tir the scribe provides the opportunity to find out what the future holds and to change it for the better.

The story that follows was taken from *100 Armenian Tales and their Folkloristic Relevance*, collected and edited by Susie Hoogasian-Villa and published by Wayne State University Press, Detroit, 1966.

Foretelling the Future

The wife of a farmer was taking care of the sheep in the fields when she gave birth to a child. A shepherd nearby saw an angel descend from heaven and write something on the baby's forehead. But since the shepherd could not see what was written, he asked the angel, "What did you do to that child?"

"I wrote his future on his forehead," the angel said.

"Why? Is he such an unusual child?"

"All human beings have their future written on their foreheads when they are born," the angel said, preparing to leave. "This child will fall from a tree and die at the age of seven."

The shepherd was very much interested: "I'll ask that woman's name, and after seven years, I will return to see if the angel's prediction comes true." And this he did.

After seven years he decided to find the woman and see how the child was. He found her house but saw that there was a large crowd gathered around it. "What has happened?" he asked a neighbor.

"The little boy who live here fell from a tree and died, and the parents want to kill the other boy who was playing with him. They say that because their son died, his playmate must die, too. Of course the playmate's parents won't permit this, and so the two families are quarreling."

"Oh, oh! The angel was right," the man said to himself, "but one death is enough. I must try to stop the second." He pushed through the crowd, went inside the house and asked the family about the trouble.

The first woman said, "My son was playing in the tree with this woman's son, and my boy fell off the tree and died. This woman's son should die, too."

"If your son fell off, why should my son die?" the second woman asked.

"Listen to me for a minute," the shepherd said. "Do you remember me?" he asked the first woman. "I am the shepherd you saw on the day your son was born in the fields. That same day, at the same time your son was born, an angel came down from heaven and wrote on his forehead. I asked the angel what he had writeen, and I was told that the little boy would fall from a tree at the age of seven and die. Now it has happened, and no one is to blame. Come, spare this little boy's life."

The first woman, seeing the truth of the argument, stopped asking for the life of the little boy. "What God has determined, we cannot prevent," she said.

***

Although many people consider divination to be a practice that goes against the grain of traditional Christian beliefs, in both the Old and New Testament we find *holy men* practising the casting of lots. It is related (Joshua 7:14 *sqq.*) that Joshua, at the Lord's command, pronounced sentence by lot on Achan who had stolen of the anathema. Again Saul, by drawing lots, found that his son Jonathan had eaten honey (1 Kings 14:58 *sqq.*). Zacharias was chosen by lot to offer incense (Luke 1:9) and the apostles by drawing lots elected Matthias to the apostleship (Acts 1:26). Therefore it would seem that divination by lots was not unlawful, at least not when practised by those who were considered to have the right to do so.

Of course we also know that in biblical times the casting of lots was commonly practised in the Middle East by peoples outside the Judaic and Christian traditions. Take the case of the mariners who transport Jonah from Joppa to Tarshish, for example, who cast lots to ascertain the cause of the evil that befalls them (Jonah 1:7).

One of the problems we are faced with when it comes to a study of divination is that despite millennia of "field testing," divination has no scientific validation. "Due to lack of controlled observations–the result of academic indifference, it is extremely difficult to refer to well organized field work on the functional outcome of divination practices. Anecdotal reports are more common but have only limited scientific value" (Frecska& Luna, 2007, p.138).

Diverging, unsystematic explanations are put forward by academics to account for the recorded successes of divination practices. On the other hand, indigenous healers of different cultures are unequivocal in their interpretation of how divination takes place, firmly and unquestionably believing it to be through the guidance of the spirits (see Frecska & Luna, 2007, p.139), and for the "insider", this is explanation enough. In any case, as "It is untenable to make statements from one form of consciousness regarding the reality of the other" (Frecska & Luna, 2007, p.143), in one sense it is a question that can never be answered to the satisfaction of all parties involved. The scientific explanation will fail to satisfy the insider, and the explanation offered by the insider will fail to satisfy the scientist.

However, if it is accepted that "the whole Universe is an inter-connected, entangled totality ... [then it has to be assumed that] consciousness is inherently nonlocal as well" (Frecska & Luna, 2007, p.148). In ASCs (altered states of consciousness) this, by all accounts, is what becomes apparent, which is why indigenous shamans induce such states for various purposes, including that of divination – to serve their communities. Neo-shamanic practi-tioners enter ASCs too, but not always to serve the community like the indigenous shaman. This is because they do not neces-sarily form part of such a clearly defined community. Consequently, there may well be times when they serve the individual rather than the group.

Either way, the breakdown of ordinary sensibility / cognition that takes place when the shaman enters ASCs is not to be seen as the ultimate goal, but rather the way to bring about healing.

What follows is a guided visualisation based on the Armenian story presented above. If you are working on your own, it is suggested that you record the script, perhaps with some appro-priate background music. You can then lie somewhere comfortable, where you will not be disturbed, and play the recording back to yourself as you go through the process described.

The Mirror that Shows your Future

SCRIPT FOR THE GUIDE: (To be read in a gentle trance-inducing voice). Make yourself comfortable and close your eyes. Take a few deep breaths to help you relax. Feel the tension disappear stage by stage from the top of your head to the tips of your toes. Let your surroundings fade away as you gradually sink backwards through time and actuality and pass through the gateway of this reality into the dreamtime. (When the participants are fully relaxed, begin the next stage).

Today's a very special day for you because you're being given an opportunity to see your future and, more importantly, to make changes now to ensure you have the best possible chance of turning it into what you want it to be.

Ahead of you what appears to be some kind of temple. Up three stone steps you make your way to an arched oak-panelled doorway. The doors are wide open for you, and within a deep blue carpet runs down the central aisle. At the end of it an indistinct figure swaying a censer perfumed with frankincense to and fro, enveloped by smoke. Breathe it in and feel centred. The smoke obscures your vision, but only temporarily, for as it clears the figure becomes clear to you – Tir the scribe and the keeper of the records. He stands by a full-length mirror. Notice both its distinct frame and shape. It shape seems to be that of a human body, your body in fact.

Tir motions to you to approach and join him, where he invites you to stand in front of the mirror and to look into it, in particular to see what is written on your forehead. And you have a minute of clock time, equal to all the time you need for this...

You're probably now wondering what you can do to change what you see. What you can do is work towards making a better future for yourself and those you interact with by learning from the mistakes you've made and by making sure you don't repeat them again. The time has come now for Tir to speak. And you have a minute of clock time, equal to all the time you need, to hear what advice he has to give you on this subject ...You can make those changes that you really wish to make, for your unconscious mind is listening and will receive and act upon the messages it hears. And you will find, as this is happening, that you become much happier, within yourself - delighted with who you are, what you have and everything you can offer. What matters now, is that you take what you have learnt back with you and that you hold on to it. The time has come to give thanks for what you have received and to take your leave, to make your way back, down the carpeted central aisle of the temple, through the arched wooden doors, down the three steps and back to the place where you started from, where your new life awaits you.

Take a deep breath, let it all out slowly, open your eyes, and smile at the first person you see. Stretch your arms, stretch your legs, stamp your feet on the ground, and make sure you're really back, back in (name of the location), back where you started from. Welcome home!

Now take a few minutes in silence to make some notes on the experiences you had on your journeys, which you can then share with the rest of the group.

Or

Now take a few minutes in silence to make some notes on the experiences you had on your journeys, which you can then make a note of in your dream journal.

Or

And now you might like to turn to the person sitting next to you and share some of the experiences you had on your journeys.

References

Berman, M. (2008) *Divination and the Shamanic Story*, Newcastle: Cambridge Scholars Publishing.

Émin, M. J. – B. (1864) *Recherches Sur Le Paganisme Arménien*, Paris: Libraire de L'Institut, de la Bibliothèque Impériale et du Sénat.

Frecska, E. & Luna, L.E. (2007) 'The Shamanic Healer: Master of Nonlocal Information.' In Shaman Vol. 15 Nos. 1 & 2.

Hoogasian-Villa, S. (1966) *100 Armenian Tales and their Folkloristic Relevance*, Detroit: Wayne State University Press.

Soul Retrieval via the Internet:
Bringing Keti Back from the Land of the Dead

Writing about shamanism has always been problematic as "the subject area resists 'objective' analysis and is sufficiently beyond mainstream research to foil ...writing about it in a conventional academic way" (Wallis, 2003, p.13). Though what follows is an example of insider research, every effort has been made to ensure that the findings "express the level of insight and constructive, critical evaluation which one's academic peers require for acceptable scholarship" (Wallis, 2003, p.6). However, we have to accept that despite our best efforts it is highly unlikely we can ever be truly objective, and this applies to both academics and practitioners alike.

It has been suggested that the only purpose of life is to know and experience God and that, in the words of the kabbalists, "God is the soul of the soul". If this is the case, it can be said that when the soul goes AWOL life loses its meaning. Soul Loss is thus the most debilitating of all illnesses and the most worthy of our consideration.

"[T]he Soul is the noblest part of man, and was given to us by God that we should nobly use it. There is no thing more precious than a human Soul, nor any earthly thing that can be weighed with it. It is worth all the gold that is in the world, and is more precious than the rubies of the kings" (from *The Fisherman and his Soul* by Oscar Wilde).

It has been suggested by Professor Paul Badham that "The main reason for studying religious experience is that it has so often been foundational for religion. Most people who believe in God do so because they have had experiences which make them think that God is real" (in 'The Case for Studying Religious Experience across Cultures and Traditions', BASR Bulletin No.112 May 2008). However, perhaps rather than religious experience being foundational for most people who believe in God or the power of the spirits, it might be more accurate to say that what it actually does is to reinforce their belief at various points in their lives. And the personal account that follows can certainly best be understood in this light.

Soul loss is the term used to describe the way parts of the psyche become detached when we are faced with traumatic situations. In psychological terms, it is known as dissociation and it works as a defence mechanism, a means of displacing unpleasant feelings, impulses or thoughts into the unconscious. In shamanic terms, these split off parts can be found in non-ordinary reality and are only accessible to those familiar with its topography (see Gagan, 1998, p.9). Soul retrieval entails the shaman journeying to find the missing parts and then returning them to the client seeking help. The shaman, in the words of Eliade, "is the great specialist in the human soul: he alone 'sees' it, for he knows its 'form' and its 'destiny'" (Eliade, 1989, p.8).

For the purposes of this study, a shaman is understood to be someone who performs an ecstatic (in a trance state), imitative, or demonstrative ritual of a séance (or a combination of all three), at will (in other words, whenever he or she chooses to do so), in which aid is sought from beings in (what are considered to be) other realities generally for healing purposes or for divination–both for individuals and / or the community.

What this suggests is that Eliade's focus on the journey as the defining feature of shamanism is not a true reflection of what actually takes place, at least not in the case of the demonstrative and imitative forms.

As for the practice of shamanism, it is understood to encompass a personalistic view of the world, in which life is seen to be not only about beliefs and practices, but also about relationships–how we are related, and how we relate to each other. And when this breaks down–in other words, when it is not taking place in a harmonious and constructive way–the shaman, employing what Graham Harvey likes to refer to as "adjusted styles of communication", makes it his or her business to resolve such issues.

One of the techniques used as a form of therapy by both indigenous and neo-shamanic practitioners alike is what is known as soul retrieval. Soul in this context can be characterized as being our vital essence, where the emotions, feelings or sentiments are situated. The aim of soul retrieval is to recover the part of the client's soul that has been lost as this causes an "opening" through which illness can enter. The cause of this loss is believed to be due to an emotional or physical trauma that the client has been through, and it is the shaman's role to track down the lost soul part in non-ordinary reality and then to return it to the body (see Ingerman, 1993, p.23).

For soul retrieval to take place, there has to be an identifiable soul to lose or to be stolen that can exist independently from the physical body. There are some who believe that "The soul, the locus of one's personal identity and characterized by mental functions like memory, allows the individual person to survive bodily corruption, remember its past life, and possibly even perceive its own unique world through such abilities as mental telepathy" (Price, 1996, p.419). There are others, however, who believe that the very idea of life after death, in a psychological rather than a physiological or biochemical sense, is unintelligible.

But why should it not be possible to suppose experiences can occur after death that are linked with experiences had before death, with our personal identities remaining intact? The problem is we can only be said to have experiences at all if we are aware of some form of world so the idea of survival in some form is dependent on there being another world or reality. H. H. Price, in his article "The Soul Survives and Functions after Death", sees this other reality as a kind of dream-world, one of mental images, which is how the world a shaman experiences when he journeys might be described by an "outsider".

However, as Price himself points out, "there is nothing imaginary about a mental image. It is an actual entity, as real as anything can be" (Price, 1996, p.422). Moreover, for those who experience it "an image world would be just as 'real' as this present world is" (Price, 1996, p.423). If we can accept what Price proposes, then the journey undertaken by the shaman for the purpose of soul recovery or retrieval becomes much easier to comprehend.

There is another argument to support the belief in some form of afterlife which perhaps should be mentioned at this point, based on a much simpler premise. A number of us (including the author of this study) have "difficulty conceiving of life without the consciousness by which we perceive it" (Leeming, 1992, p.65) and, as far as such people are concerned, this is justification enough. And of course "no one can ever fully realize the fact of his own death, which is fundamentally as inconceivable as the fact of not having been before one's own birth" (Frankl, 1986, p.138).

And to give further support to the case being made, the words of Aua, a Hudson Bay Eskimo and shaman interviewed by Rasmussen, are worth quoting in full:

We ignorant Eskimos living up here do not believe, as you have told us many white men do, in one great solitary spirit that from a place far up in the sky maintains humanity and all the life of nature. Among us, as I have already explained to you, all is bound up with the earth we live on and our life here: and it would be even more incomprehensible, even more unreasonable, if, after a life short or long, of happy days or of suffering and misery, we were then to cease all together from existence. What we have heard about the soul shows us that the life of men and beasts does not end with death. When, at the end of life, we draw our last breath, that is not the end. We awake to consciousness again, we come to life again, and all this is effected through the medium of the soul. Therefore is it that we regard the soul as the greatest and most incomprehensible of all. (Rasmussen, 1930, pp.60-61).

What follows is an account of a soul retrieval that was carried out over the internet by the shamanic practitioner Jonathan Horwitz over a period of two weeks between December 2006 and January 2007 to bring my partner Keti back from the Land of the Dead after she had an aneurism, was in a coma, and after a priest had been called to deliver the last rites.

First of all, however, to give some idea of what soul retrieval entails, here are a couple of extracts from an account of the procedure:

For a soul retrieval, I will ask Anne to let down next to me on my rug in the small room in which I work. I will touch her at the shoulder, hip, and ankle so that the psychic connection between the two of us is strong. I use a tape of drumming so that my own free soul can leave my body and search for Anne's soul ... I pulled that part from non-ordinary reality into ordinary reality and proceeded to blow the soul back into Anne's heart center and then, after sitting her up, into the crown of her head (Ingerman, 1993, pp.25 & 29).

The process does not end at this point because it is re-enforced with follow-up work:

Once the healing is performed, the next step is for the client to start to look at life after illness, a process that involves two very crucial questions: What changes do I need to create in my life that will keep me healthy? How do I want to use my creative energy to make something positive in my life? (Ingerman, 1993, p.35).

The neo-shamanic soul retrieval process will clearly vary from practitioner to practitioner. Generally speaking, however, it consists of a series of encounters between shaman and client. At the initial meeting the practitioner tells the client about the theory of soul loss and the client explains why he or she wants to undergo the treatment. For the actual soul retrieval, the client is generally asked to lie on the floor, close his / her eyes and relax, while the shaman, lying next to the client, goes into a trance and journeys into non-ordinary reality to find the lost soul part and bring it back. On the return to ordinary reality, the practitioner then blows the soul part into the client's chest and into the top of the head. This done, the shaman tells the client what happened on the journey and the client relates to this by putting the shaman's images into the context of his / her own experience. The last stage in the sequence is for the client to journey back to the time and place of the original loss, and to communicate with the soul part about why it left and the conditions under which it agreed to return, and the client is then expected to comply with these conditions.

One of the numerous roles that the shaman has always been required to perform, in both indigenous and now in neo-shamanism, is as the person who is called upon when emergency strikes–physical or spiritual. Indeed, certain alternative practitioners would even go so far as to suggest that the former is in any case nothing more than a symptom of the latter. Take the case of my partner, for example, a non-believer in shamanism and a devout Orthodox Christian, who had an aneurism while in transit at Vienna airport and who was rushed by ambulance to hospital. There she was operated on immediately and by the time I had flown in from London to be by her side, she had already been placed in an induced coma to protect her from any further complications and was lying in an intensive care unit. As for her chances of recovery, I was told by the surgeon who had operated on her that realistically they were extremely low.

Prior to the crisis, there had been a lot of conflict between me and my partner's children (my stepchildren) and this had caused Keti (my partner) considerable distress. Indeed, so much so that it could well have been a contributing factor to what ensued.

In desperation (and by e-mail as this was my only means of contacting him at the time), I turned to the shamanic practitioner (and my teacher) Jonathan Horwitz, who had never met Keti and who knew nothing about her except for the nature of her illness, and this was his response:

Dear Michael,

A very powerful helper has arrived at the scene, a Chestnut Mare. If it is possible for Ketevan to understand this beautiful mystic practise we call shamanism, please ask her to open herself up to this power of the Chestnut Mare. This Helper may even already have a meaning for her. Ask her to let the Chestnut Mare into her dreams. And keep me in touch.

Love to you both,

Jonathan

This was followed by Jonathan carrying out a soul retrieval for Keti despite the fact that he was in an extremely remote region of Sweden at the time. A copy of the e-mail he then sent me, summarising what he found, is presented below:

Dear Michael!

Unfortunately I left your telephone number at my place in Sweden! Please send it to me, along with the best times to ring to you.

How are you? I have been thinking about you both and praying for you. I did a soul retrieval immediately after we talked. She was standing right next to her body and looked ready to leave. I pleaded with her to get back into her body and said that the situation would be different if she returned, and she wouldn't be feeling the need to leave. Finally she agreed to reenter her body, but she didn't seem convinced, but she did it with sort of a "Well, here goes...." feeling.

I am back in Copenhagen now at ....

Much Love to you,

Jonathan

As for Keti, she woke up the very same day it was received. The "outsider" could justifiably argue this was nothing more than a coincidence, though the "insider" would clearly not share this view. What has been described here, in effect, is a story in the Orpheus tradition:

The story, which generally involves a human married couple (and thus may be termed a tale), but sometimes portrays the relationship between a god and his consort (and thus should be called a myth) varies, naturally, from culture to culture, but usually expresses one central theme: a loving husband's pursuit of his deceased young wife as her soul steers toward the land of the dead. Sometimes he succeeds in bringing her back to life, sometimes, like the Greek Orpheus, he does not, and this is the most common version. The tale is ... evidently built on the experiences of the shaman who discharges his soul to the realm of the dead in order to fetch a sick person's soul (Hultkrantz, 1993, p.44).

One of the criticisms levelled against neo-shamanism is that the indigenous cosmological world ends up becoming detached from the environmental and social context which it is part of, and "imbued instead with Jungian archetypes; the 'teacher within', the process of 'individuation', an 'inner landscape'. Rather the travelling into a 'real' spirit world, neo-Shamanic journeys are often perceived as being trips into oneself" (Wallis,

2003, p.59). Soul Loss similarly gets devalued, with the assumption being that it involves healing emotional wounds rather than the actual retrieval of someone's lost soul or soul part. It does not have to be regarded in this light, though, and it certainly was not in this particular case.

It should perhaps be pointed out that this account has not been presented here to prove or disprove the power of shamanism. The reason for offering it to you is rather to show what a crucial role the shaman still has to play, even in the lives of sophisticated urbanites, and how the role has evolved to suit the times we are now living in—with soul retrievals even being carried out via the worldwide web.

It is generally agreed that part of the healing process is being able to put a name to whatever condition a patient is suffering from, and that naming an inauspicious condition is halfway to removing it. Embodying the invisible in a tangible symbol, such as that of soul theft, can be regarded as a big step towards remedying it and, as Turner (1995) points out, is not so far removed from the practice of the modern psychoanalyst. Once something is grasped by the mind, it can then be dealt with and mastered. Thus the goal of therapy is not only to cure but also to give meaning to sickness. However, it has been suggested that something else is required first before the healing process can take effect because "not only must the disease be named, but the diagnosis must reflect the shared world view of healer and client to be effective" (Villoldo & Krippner, 1987, p.193). This is because when the world view of the practitioner is not shared by the client, then the client clearly has less reason to be as committed to the process as he / she might otherwise be, and his / her expectation of recovery will be adversely affected too.

On the other hand, not everyone would necessarily agree with Volloldo and Krippner. It has been suggested that "By performing a liturgical order the participants accept, and indicate to themselves and to others that they accept whatever is encoded in the canon of that order" (Rappaport, 1999, p.119) provided, of course, they are not acting. Though acceptance can be regarded as intrinsic to liturgical performance it should not be confused with belief. For acceptance is a public act whereas belief is a private state (see Rappaport, 1999, pp.119-120). It is interesting to note in this respect that "Judaism does not require the devout to believe, for belief is not subject to demand. It does, however, demand of them that they *accept* the law, and this acceptance is signalled by, and is intrinsic to, conformity to the ritual observances that pervade all of life" (Rappaport, 1999, p.120). However, is acceptance really enough or is belief required too in order to gain the maximum possible benefit from the sort of rituals we are concerned with in this work?

Let me answer the question like this. I believe Keti's soul retrieval was brought about by shamanic intervention. However, as far as Keti is concerned, it was brought about by the prayers said over her by a Georgian Orthodox priest who visited the hospital. But considering both rituals took place while she was in a coma, it would seem that neither acceptance nor belief is necessarily required on the part of the patient in order for the process to be effective – and that what is required in effect is a miracle for what happened cannot be explained any other way. In this particular case, however, as the supernatural event occurred with, rather than without, mortal intervention, it could well be argued that sorcery would be a more accurate term to describe what took place.

The story that follows offers a stark warning to anyone who wastes the second chance they have been given to have the person they love returned to them. It was taken from *The Religion of the Luiseño Indians of Southern California* by Constance Goddard DuBois, a primary source of information on the religious beliefs and practices of the Luiseño people, who resided in what is now North San Diego and Orange counties in California.

The Spirit Wife

Some years ago the people from the Potrero district used to go up to an old village site on Palomar mountain, Pahamuk, near where Bailey's place is now, at the season for gathering acorns; and while they still lived there, a young man abused his wife. He scolded and beat her all the time, and she was always sad. She got sick and did not want to live. She would rather die. She had a little baby boy just beginning to crawl. Soon the woman died, and the man was left alone with his baby. He had to carry the baby about with him all the time, and the baby cried. The man went up the mountain to gather acorns, and left the baby lying under a tree. The baby cried and cried, until at last the spirit of the mother came and took the baby in her arms. The man came down the mountain and found the woman there. She spoke to him and said that he had been so cruel to her that she had had to leave him; but that now he must never be unkind to her again. She had come back to him because he and the baby were suffering without her. She could stay with him as long as he was kind to her, but no longer. So he promised never to treat her harshly again.She used to make the wiwish, acorn mush; but it was never good. It was always watery. The man was sure he would never abuse his wife again. But when she made the mush just as she used to, and it was thin, he acted as before and lifted his hand to beat her."You promised not to be angry," she said, "but now you are doing the same as formerly. I see that you cannot be trusted to be good. So now I shall have to leave you." With this she turned into a dove and flew away. The man fell on his back; and he and his baby stayed alone.

As for the secret of how to hold on to love and your partner once you get him or her back, perhaps it lies in the Ainu folktale of *The Man who lost his Wife*. The Ainu are an ethnic minority in Japan, living primarily on the northernmost Japanese island of Hokkaidō. Ainu literature was traditionally of an exclusively oral variety, and very little was reduced to writing in any language before the 19th century. Many of the stories occur in more or less lengthy poems known as *yukar*, which are an epic-like form. Basil Hall Chamberlain, the translator of this particular story, was well-known as one of the pioneering translators and interpreters of things Japanese in his time. (He also translated the Shinto classic *Kojiki*.)

The Man who lost his Wife

A man had lost his wife, and was searching for her everywhere, over hill and dale, forest and sea-shore. At last he came to a wide plain, on which stood an oak-tree. Going up to it he found it to be not so much an oak-tree as a house, in which dwelt a kind-looking old man. Said the old man: "'I am the god of the oak-tree. I know of your loss, and have seen your faithful search. Rest here awhile, and refresh yourself by eating and smoking. After that, if you hope to find your wife again, you must obey my orders, which are as follows: Take this golden horse, get on his back, fly up on him to the sky, and, when you get there, ride about the streets, constantly singing."

So the man mounted the horse, which was of pure gold. The saddle and all the trappings were of gold also. As soon as he was in the saddle, the horse flew up to the sky. There the man found a world like ours, but more beautiful. There was an immense city in it; and up and down the streets of that city, day after day, he rode, singing all the while. Every one in the sky stared at him, and all the people put their hands to their noses, saying: "How that creature from the lower world stinks!" At last the stench became so intolerable to them that the chief god of the sky came and told him that he should be made to find his wife if only he would go away. Thereupon the man flew back to earth on his golden horse. Alighting at the foot of the oak-tree, he said to the oak-god: "Here am I. I did as you bade me. But I did not find my wife." "Wait a moment," said the oak-god; "you do not know what a tumult has been caused by your visit to the sky, neither have I yet told you that it was a demon who stole your wife. This demon, looking up from hell below, was so much astonished to see and hear you riding up and down the streets of heaven singing, that his gaze is still fixed in that direction. I will profit hereby to go round quietly, while his attention is absorbed, and let your wife out of the box in which he keeps her shut up."

The oak-god did as he had promised. He brought back the woman, and handed over both her and the gold horse to the man, saying: "Do not use this horse to make any more journeys to the sky. Stay on earth, and breed from it." The couple obeyed his commands, and became very rich. The gold horse gave birth to two horses, and these two bred likewise, till at last horses filled all the land of the Ainos.—(Written down from memory. Told by Ishanashte, 21st July, 1886)

***

To conclude, what I would suggest that Keti's "soul retrieval" shows is that "No religious behaviour, however archaic it may be, is ever definitively abolished. An in-depth crisis, a syncretism inspired by despair, can make any divinity real, whether it be exotic or peripheral" (Eliade, 1977, p.154).

References

Badham, P. (2008) 'The Case for Studying Religious Experience across Cultures and Traditions', in BASR Bulletin No.112.

Berman, M. (2008) *Soul Loss and the Shamanic Story*, Newcastle: Cambridge Scholars Publishing.

Chamberlain, B.H. (1888) Aino Folk-tales, London. {reduced to HTML by Christopher M. Weimer August 2002.} Scanned at sacred-texts.com. Edited and Proofed by John Bruno Hare. This text is in the public domain in the United States because it was published prior to January 1st, 1923. These files may be used for any non-commercial purpose provided this notice of attribution is left intact in all copies.

DuBois, C.G. (1908) *The Religion of the Luiseño Indians of Southern California*, Berkeley: The University Press, University of California Publications, Department of Anthropology. [Scanned, proofed and formatted by John Bruno Hare at sacred-texts.com, April 2008. This text is in the public domain in the US because it was published prior to 1923].

Eliade, M. (1977) *No Souvenirs: Journal 1957-1969*, San Francisco: Harper & Row Publishers (originally published in France as *Fragments d'un journal* in 1973).

Eliade, M. (1989) *Shamanism: Archaic techniques of ecstasy*, London: Arkana (first published in the USA by Pantheon Books 1964).

Frankl, V.E.(1986) *The Doctor and the Soul: From Psychotherapy to Logotherapy*, New York: Vintage Books.

Gagan, J.M. (1998) *Journeying: where shamanism and psychology meet*, Santa Fe, NM: Rio Chama Pubications.

Horwitz, J. 'Coming Home: The Shaman's Work with Soul-Loss.' http://www.shamanism.dk/Articles.html   [accessed 12/11/06].

Hultkrantz, A. (1993) 'The Shaman in Myths and Tales.' In *Shaman*, Vol. 1 No.2. Autumn 1993.

Ingerman, S. (1991) *Soul Retrieval: Mending the Fragmented Self through Shamanic Practice*, San Francisco: Harper.

—. (1993) *Welcome Home: Following Your Soul's Journey Home*, New York: Harper Collins Publishers.

Leeming, D.A., (1990) *The World of Myth*, New York: Oxford University Press.

Price, H.H. (1996) 'The Soul Survives and Functions after Death.' In Michael Peterson, William Hasker, Bruce Reichenbach, and David Basinger (eds.) *Philosophy of Religion: Selected Readings*, New York: Oxford University Press. Pp.447-456.

Rappaport, R.A. (1999) *Ritual and Religion in the Making of*

Humanity, Cambridge: Cambridge University Press.

Rasmussen, K. (1930) *Intellectual Culture of the Hudson Bay Eskimos*, Copenhagen: Gyldendalske Boghandel, Nordisk Forlag.

Turner, V. (1995) *The Ritual Process: Structure and Anti-Structure*, Chicago, Illinois: Aldine Publishing Company (first published in 1969).

Villoldo, A., & Krippner, S. (1987) *Healing States: A Journey into the World of Spiritual Healing and Shamanism*, New York: Fireside.

Wallis, Robert J. (2003) *Shamans/Neo-Shamans: Ecstasy, Alternative Archaeologies and Contemporary Pagans*, London: Routledge.

The Circassians and the Shamanic Elements in their Folktales

The Republic of Adygeya is situated on the picturesque northern slopes of the Caucasian ridge descending to the fertile plain of the Kuban River, and was on the legendary Silk Route. More than eighty nationalities live in the republic, a territory of just 7,800 kilometres, with Adyghs and Russians constituting the two major ethnic groups, and the capital is the city of Maykop.On one website Adygeya is described as a "genuine tourist paradise", though it is probably best to take this with a pinch of salt, as is the case with most such descriptions:

Magnificent foothills of the Caucasus, the beautiful Lagonaki Plateau, the abundance of karst caves, snow mountain caps, luxuriant Alpine meadows, wide steppes, century-old trees, mountain rivers with water-falls, and quiet lakes - that is what rapturous travelers are going to see if they come to Adygeya (http://www.adygnet.ru/english/aboutadyg/aboutadygheya.shtml [accessed 9/11/09]).The Adyghe do not only inhabit Adygeya (a constituent republic of the Russian Federation since 1991), but also Karachay-Cherkessia where they are known as "Cherkes." There are also the Kabardin of Kabardino-Balkaria, along with the Besleney tribe, who are often conceived as the eastern branch of the Adyghe. While Adyghe is the name this people apply to themselves, in the West they are often known as the Circassians. Their language is referred to as Adyghe or Adygeyan, a member of the Northwast Caucasian (Circassian) language family though most Adyghe also speak Russian, and both languages are written with the Cyrillic alphabet. The total population, including the Circassian diaspora, is about 2.9 million and their religion is mainly Sunni Islam.

The Adyghe first emerged as a coherent entity somewhere around the tenth century A.D., though references to them exist much earlier. However, they were never politically united, which reduced their influence in the area and also their ability to withstand the periodic invasions they were subject to from groups like the Mongols, Avars, Pechenegs, Huns, and Khazars. Eventually this lack of unity cost the Adyghe their independence to Russia in 1864. Like other ethnic minorities under Russian rule, the policies of mass resettlement caused the people a great deal of suffering, and collectivization under the communists also took its toll. In fact, the Russian conquest led to the exodus of almost 90% of all Circassians to the Ottoman Empire, and it was such a cataclysmic event that it nearly resulted in their extinction. Their land was then colonised by the Cossacks and Russians and the bulk of the population of Adygeya today are the descendants of these colonists. This has resulted in making the republic demographically the most "Russianized" national unit of the whole Northern Caucasus

Beslenet (2002) argues that by creating conditions of positive discrimination for the Adyge minority and its language, which has long suffered from the *imperialist conquest and colonisation of the 19ᵗʰ Century*, local Russians who want to hold governmental posts will have an incentive to learn the language of the titular nation- a decision which may even pave the way in the end for an Adyge speaker of Russian majority to become president. He believes this could result in Adygeya putting aside its ethnic problems and instead concentrating on implementing economic reforms and creating a democratic, prosperous society where the particularities of the Adyge are also respected alongside the wider republican population and taken into consideration. It remains to be seen, however, whether this will actually take place.

As for the people and their way of life,

the Circassian are largely a rural people. Their traditional economy is based on herding and farming, supplemented by growing fruit. They also raise chickens, cows, sheep, goats, pigs, and especially horses. They grow a variety of grains, and in the highlands, they also hunt. They eat bread, milk, cheese, broth, fruit and vegetable dishes, and occasionally, a meat dish with a spicy nut sauce.

Traditionally, Circassian houses were spaced fairly far apart along a river, generally in the higher country. The dwelling, called a *wuna*, was a long rectangular house with a porch extending along its front. It was made of twigs coated with mud and had a thatch roof. There were several rooms, including at least one for the women. The house usually had a large tree planted in front of its door to symbolize the growth and strength of the family. A vegetable garden and several other houses (for sons and their families), as well as buildings for livestock and food storage were located behind the main house. The entire compound was enclosed in a stockade. Today, [however,] in the lowland villages where most of the people live, standardized brick homes with garden plots have replaced traditional patterns. ...

Outside of the cities, the extended family is the most common unit, sometimes containing as many as four or five generations. Members of a *tlapq* (clan) are descended from the same male ancestors and share a common name. Marriages are based on love or mutual interest and occur when the couple is in their early thirties. The wife has authority over many of the household matters, but the husband has the final say in disputes. A man was traditionally never without his dagger, and few things were more important to him than his weapons. This reflected the prevalence of the "blood feud" (Joshua Project http://www.joshuaproject.net/peopctry.php?rop3=100079&rog3=RS [accessed 13/11/09]).

The pre-colonial Adyghe were warriors in a matriarchal society where women and men fought side by side. Since Russian colonisation the matriarchy has been destroyed, although elements of it still remain in Adyghe culture and society, in which women are highly respected and honoured, such as the Ceremony of the Puppet Princess described below.

What soon becomes apparent on visiting the region is that although the Adyghe, when questioned, might describe themselves as Moslems, in reality they follow an eclectic mix of traditions that include pagan practices too.

Hantse Guashe, the Ceremony of the Puppet Princess, known as Dzivara among the Abkhazians, is a pagan ritual for rain still performed today in the region. The puppet must have originally represented the figure of the mother goddess Khuhabe (Къу - бабэ), a symbol of fertility. Versions of the ceremony can also be found among the different tribes of the Circassians. The Shapsyghs would hold the Hantse Guashe in the river till it began to rain. As written by Kashej Talip, Kabardeys would stand the Hantse Guashe in the middle of the village and dance around it with their traditional dance Wuic Xhurey. Another version has been founding among another Adyghe group who would carry the Hantse Guashe with cheese and flour inside a sieve, in which the whey symbolized the rain and the flour symbolised fertile soil (see Dumanish Auledin, *Çerkes Kültürü Üzerine Etüd*, Kayseri Kafkas Derneği, 2004).

The Kabardian tale that follows is from Adolf Dirr's 1925 collection, *Caucasian Folk-tales*, translated into English by Lucy Menzies.

The Courageous Daughter

An old nobleman had three daughters but no sons. One day it occurred to him that he might test the courage of his daughters. To this end he ordered the eldest to dress herself in men's clothes, to mount a horse and set out to seek adventure. But he himself lurked under a bridge she had to cross. As she rode over it, he sprang out and pretended he was about to seize her; she was so frightened that she swooned and fell from her horse.

The following day he sent his second daughter out. He waited for her too, and as he seized her, her horse took fright and she fell, like her sister, in a swoon.

Then he sent his youngest daughter. Again he lay in wait under the bridge, sprang out suddenly and seized her. The horse was frightened and shied to the side, but the rider held it with a firm hand and gave her assailant such a blow with her riding-whip that it cost him his little finger. In spite of the pain her father rejoiced in her courage, let her go and returned home himself. After she had crossed the bridge the maiden rode straight on. Whether she travelled far or not – who knows? But at laast she came to a town.

"What is the news here?" she asked the first person she met.

"Only this," she was answered, "that our Chan wishes to set free, for his son, a certain maiden who is watched over by many spirits. No one can be found to undertake this task."

But the unknown knight pleased all the people so much by his bearing (she was dressed, remember, like a man), that they asked him to attempt to set the maiden free. And after many requests, the unknown horseman agreed.

She set out on her search. On the way she passed over a burning plain, where she found three young serpents trying to escape from the flames. She lifted them up with her riding-switch and so saved them. When she had left the burning plain behind, she set the little creatures down on the ground and rode after them without allowing herself to lose sight of them. The serpents crawled towards a kurgan (a great artificial burial mound). As they drew near it, it opened up, and the maiden went in after the serpents. Now the mound housed a good spirit, the mother of the three young serpents. "I have three young ones every year," she said, "but I always lose them through the burning of the plain. Had you not been there, I had lost these three also. There is nothing I would not do for you. Tell me, what do you want?"

"For myself, I want nothing. But I am looking for a certain maiden. Help me to find her."

"That is not difficult," answered the mother of the young serpents, "only you will never get there on that horse. Take this black horse rather. When you come to the place, hide yourself behind the house and lie in wait till the maiden goes out. The leap with your horse over the hedge, and when he kneels down, seize the maiden and ride – as hard as you can. No one will overtake you, and you can return home in safety."

So the maiden mounted the black steed and set out. She did everything as she had been told; in spite of all the shouts of the watchman, she brought the stolen maiden safely away. When she got to the town of the Chan for whom she had undertaken this task, the maiden said to her: "I will only sign the marriage deeds if the box with seven locks is brought to me which is wrapped up in a dog-skin in a secret room." And so our heroine turned again to the mother of the serpents for advice. "If you want to carry out this task," she said, "then you must ride there on a grey horse, When you come near the house, touch the doors with this little stick; they will then open of themselves, and when you seize the dog-skin, it also will open of itself. The take the box and ride back."

The heroine did all this as she was told. But still the bride, although she now had her box, would hear nothing of marriage. "There dwell in the sea," she said, "a buffalo ox and seven buffalo cows. Bring them here to me and milk the cows. Then boil the milk and pour it hot into a trough. I will jump in from one side and swim through it, while he who wants to marry me must jump in at the other side. If he also swims through, then I agree to marry him; but if not, then I refuse."

Our heroine set out on her travels once more. The mother of

the serpents said to her: "take a dun horse this time and ride to the sea-shore. When you get there roll yourself and your horse in the black sand, then ride into the sea. Wherever the buffalo may be, your dun horse will find them. Only take care not to fall from your horse when the buffalo attacks you." The heroine carried out all these directions faithfully. The buffalo seized her, but she drove it to the shore. Then it cursed her – and the curse of a buffalo is always fulfilled. "Whosoever drives us out of the sea shall become a woman if he is a man, and a man if she is a woman," he bellowed. And in truth our heroine changed at that moment into a man. And when he had driven the buffalo cows home, he had them milked and the milk heated. It was poured into a trough, the bride threw herself into it from one side, the son of the Chan from the other. He was boiled to pieces in the hot milk and his body had to be fished out. But the bride swam through.

"The Chan's son is dead," cried all the people. "He who fetched the bride shall have her now."

And so it happened, and they lived happily and contented ever after.

***

The shamanic story can be defined as a story that has either been based on or inspired by a shamanic journey, or one that contains a number of the elements typical of such a journey. Like other genres, it has "its own style, goals, entelechy, rhetoric, developmental pattern, and characteristic roles" (Turner, 1985, p.187), and like other genres it can be seen to differ to a certain extent from culture to culture. It should perhaps be noted at this point, however, that there are both etic and emic ways of regarding narrative (see Turner, 1982, p.65) and the term "shamanic story" clearly presents an outside view. It should also be pointed out that what is being offered here is a polytheistic definition of what the shamanic story is, in which a pool of characteristics can apply, but need not.

Characteristics typical of the genre include the way in which the stories all tend to contain embedded texts (often the account of the shamanic journey itself), how the number of actors is clearly limited as one would expect in subjective accounts of what can be regarded as inner journeys, and how the stories tend to be used for healing purposes.

In his Foreword to *Tales of the Sacred and the Supernatural*, Eliade admits to repeatedly taking up "the themes of *sortie du temps*, or temporal dislocation, and of the alteration or the transmutation of space" (Eliade, 1981, p.10), and these are themes that appear over and over again in shamanic stories too[1].

Additionally, given that through the use of narrative shamans are able to provide their patients "with a language, by means of which unexpressed, and otherwise inexpressible, psychic states can be expressed" (Lévi-Strauss, 1968, p.198), it follows that another feature of shamanic stories is they have the potential to provide the same too.

They are also frequently examples of what Jürgen Kremer, transpersonal psychologist and spiritual practitioner, called "tales of power" after one of Carlos Castaneda's novels. He defines such texts as 'conscious verbal constructions based on numinous experiences in non-ordinary reality, "which guide individuals and help them to integrate the spiritual, mythical, or archetypal aspects of their internal and external experience in unique, meaningful, and fulfilling ways" (Kremer, 1988, p.192). In other words, they can serve the purpose of helping us reconnect with our indigenous roots.

The style of storytelling most frequently employed in both shamanic stories and in fairy tales is that of magic realism, in which although "the point of departure is 'realistic' (recognizable events in chronological succession, everyday atmosphere, verisimilitude, characters with more or less predictable psychological reactions), ... soon strange discontinuities or gaps appear in the 'normal,' true-to-life texture of the narrative" (Calinescu, 1978, p.386). In other words, what happens is that our expectations based on our intuitive knowledge of physics are ultimately breached and knocked out. It is, in effect, very much the style of storytelling that we find in *The Courageous Daughter*.

When it comes to the interpretation of any folktale, however, we need to keep in mind that every written text is no less an act of creating a new reality than of describing a given one. Consequently, there is no way in which any conclusions that are drawn about the way in which the tale reflects the lives and practices of the people at the time it relates to can be regarded as hard facts. And for this reason, all we can do, in effect, is to make educated guesses about such matters. At the same time, however, it should also be pointed out that absence of evidence is not evidence of absence either.

What we find in this particular tale, more or less right from the start, is the breakthrough between the planes that accompanies the shamanic process

The shamanic journey frequently involves passing through some kind of gateway. As Eliade explains, The "clashing of rocks," the "dancing reeds," the gates in the shape of jaws, the "two razor-edged restless mountains," the "two clashing icebergs," the "active door," the "revolving barrier," the door made of the two halves of the eagle's beak, and many more – all these are images used in myths and sagas to suggest the insurmountable difficulties of passage to the Other World [and sometimes the passage back too] (Eliade, 2003, pp.64-65). And to make such a journey requires a change in one's mode of being, entering a transcendent state, which makes it possible to attain the world of spirit. (Berman, 2007, p.48).

In the case of *The Courageous Daughter*, initially the gateway is represented by the bridge that has to be crossed, and also by the burning plain.

It is at this point that a stylistic device which can be found in many folktales from the region is employed. "Whether she travelled far or not – who knows?" What we learn from this is that time and distance can no longer be measured in the conventional way, and that we have entered non-ordinary reality by this stage.

The number three plays an important part in the story, with there being three sisters, three serpents, and three horses too. Not only does the number three appear in many folktales, (three brothers or sisters, three tasks to accomplish, three encounters, three guesses, three little pigs, three bears), but it also has mystical and spiritual associations. In ancient Babylon the three primary gods were Anu, Bel (Baal), and Ea, representing Heaven, Earth, and the Abyss. Similarly, there were three aspects to the Egyptian sun god: Khepri (rising), Re (midday), and Atum (setting). And in Christianity there is the Trinity of God the Father, God the Son, and God the Holy Spirit.

The Pythagoreans believed that man is a full chord, or eight notes, and deity comes next. Three is the perfect trinity and represents perfect unity, twice three is the perfect dual, and three times three is the perfect plural, which explains why nine was considered to be a mystical number. Our tale certainly has a mystical element to it, and its connection to such symbolism clearly gives it greater significance. However, to suggest that the comparison with a trinity of trinities was intentional on the part of its author is perhaps, though interesting, a bit too far-fetched. One of the problems when it comes to considering symbolism is symbolic meaning can be read into almost anything and there is often no way of checking the interpretation.

As for the horses, the fact that the animal plays a significant role in the story should come as no surprise to anyone familiar with both the geography and history of the region. "The human-horse relationship is clearly an important one 'in a region with extensive uninhabited areas, in which one's horse may have literally meant the difference between life and death" (Dolidze, 1999, p.9), and the connection felt between mountaineer and horse in the Caucasus is probably as ancient as their myths. There is, for example, a Georgian legend that asks, "Who were my ancestors?" And the answer given is "He who pulled milk out of a wild mare's udder with his lips and grew drunk as a little foal". The horse is also frequently the form of transport used by the shaman to access other worlds.

> The "horse" is employed by the shaman, in various contexts, as a means of achieving ecstasy, that is, the "coming out of oneself" that makes the mystical journey possible. ... The horse carries the deceased into the beyond; it produces the "break-through in plane," the passage from this world to other worlds (Eliade, 1964, p.467).

According to Yakut beliefs, the horse is of divine origin. In the beginning God is said to have created a horse from which a half horse-half man descended, and from this being humankind was born. The Sky-Horse deity, Uordakh-Djesegei, plays a major role in Yakut religion, and Yakut mythology depicts many other scenes in which deities and guardian spirits descend to the earth as horses. The honourable goddess Ajjyst, the patron of child-bearing, appears as a white mare, as does the goddess called Lajahsit. The horse is of great significance to the shaman too. "A Yakut shaman's healing performance is unthinkable without a horse, just as the entire ceremony cannot occur without the shaman's participation ... A horse, its image, or at times, an object personifying the animal is always present in the shaman's preparations and performances" (Diachenko, 1994, p.266).

Among Turkic-speaking people of South Siberia, including Tuvinians, the horse can play an important role too, and it is the drum that can represent the animal ridden by shamans to travel to other worlds. Its handle can be regarded as the horse's "spine;the plaits of leather attached to the upper part of the ring symbolize the reins of the horse; the drumstick is a lash, which beats a drum only in certain places" (Diakonova, 1994, p.253

The number seven also features prominently in the story, in that the box has seven locks and there are seven buffalo cows. The number seven, like the number three, is also mystic or sacred number in many different traditions. Among the Babylonians and Egyptians, there were believed to be seven planets, and the alchemists recognized seven planets too. In the Old Testament there are seven days in creation, and for the Hebrews every seventh year was Sabbatical too. There are seven virtues, seven sins, seven ages in the life of man, seven wonders of the world, and the number seven repeatedly occurs in the Apocalypse as well. The Muslims talk of there being seven heavens, with the seventh being formed of divine light that is beyond the power of words to describe, and the Kabbalists also believe there are seven heavens – each arising above the other, with the seventh being the abode of God. So seven is surely not an arbitrary number plucked out of the blue, but included in the tale for a reason.

Although the cosmology, described in Creation Myths, will vary from culture to culture, the structure of the whole cosmos is frequently symbolized by the number seven ..., which is made up of the four directions, the centre, the zenith in heaven, and the nadir in the underworld. The essential axes of this structure are the four cardinal points and a central vertical axis passing through their point of intersection that connects the Upper World, the Middle World and the Lower World. The names by which the central vertical axis that connects the three worlds is referred to include the world pole, the tree of life, the sacred mountain, the central house pole, and Jacob's ladder (Berman, 2007, p.45).

When the youngest daughter enters the *kurgan*, what she is in effect doing is entering the Lower World, and it is there that she finds a Spirit Helper to aid her in her quest, in the form of the mother of the serpents. As for the horses, they are a traditional means of transport for shamans to travel to other realities on. And finally our heroine shape-shifts from a woman into a man, as a result of which balance is restored to the community once more. Although these days the neo-shamanic practitioner often works primarily to serve the needs of individual clients, the role of the indigenous shaman was more to do with maintaining the equilibrium of the whole community, and this is what the youngest daughter can be seen to re-establish in this tale.

The ability to shape-shift is one of the attributes often credited to shamans, and it is not only shamans who have such powers according to tales from around the globe. Shape shifting is part of a mythic and story-telling tradition stretching back over thousands of years. In Nordic myth, Odin could change his shape into any beast or bird; in Greek myth, Zeus often assumed animal shape in his relentless pursuit of young women. Cernunnos, the lord of animals in Celtic mythology, wore the shape of a stag, and also the shape of a man with a heavy rack of horns.

With shape-shifting, a journey into non-ordinary reality, descent to the Lower World, a meeting with a spirit helper, a quest entailing various ordeals that can be regarded as a process of initiation for our heroine to see whether she is worthy to eventually take on the role that her father had previously performed, what we have here is essentially a shamanic story rather than what at first sight might appear to be just a simple fairy tale, and the same can be shown to be the case with many other tales from the Caucasus.

"Sceptics will argue that it is impossible to eliminate from analysis the [Islamic and] Christian influence on what sources there are available to us, such that we can never be certain in any one case that we are indeed dealing with beliefs that are authentically pagan. This view is now so widely held that we can in justice think of it as the prevailing orthodoxy" (Winterbourne, 2007, p.24). And the same argument could be applied to the attempt to ascertain whether we are dealing with beliefs that are authentically shamanic in *The Courageous Daughter.* Nevertheless, just because a task is difficult is no reason for not attempting it. If it was, then no progress would ever be made in any research that we might be involved in. For this reason, despite whatever the prevailing orthodoxy might be, it there is surely every reason to conduct such a study as this.

References

Auledin, D. (2004) *Çerkes Kültürü Üzerine Etüd,* Kayseri Kafkas Derneği.

Berman, M. (2007) *The Nature of Shamanism and the Shamanic Story,* Newcastle: Cambridge Scholars Publishing.

Berman, M. (2008) *Divination and the Shamanic Story,* Newcastle: Cambridge Scholars Publishing.

Besleney, Z. A. (2002) 'A Country Study: The Republic of Adygeya' http://www.kafkas.org.tr/english/analiz/Policy_of_positive_discr imination_for_the_titular_nation_in_Adygeya_.htm [accessed 10/11/09]).

Calinescu, M. (1978) 'The Disguises of Miracle: Notes on Mircea Eliade's Fiction.' In Bryan Rennie (ed.) (2006) *Mircea Eliade: A Critical Reader,* London: Equinox Publishing Ltd.

Diachenko, V. (1994) 'The Horse in Yakut Shamanism' In Seaman, G., & Day, J.S. *Ancient Traditions: Shamanism in Central Asia and the Americas,* Boulder, Colorado: University Press of Colorado.

Diakonova, V.P. (1994) 'Shamans in Traditional Tuvinian Society' In Seaman, G., & Day, J.S. *Ancient Traditions: Shamanism in Central Asia and the Americas,* Boulder, Colorado: University Press of Colorado.

Dirr, A. (1925) *Caucasian Folk-tales*, London & Toronto: J.M. Dent & Sons Ltd.

Dolidze, N.I. (1999) *Georgian Folktales*, Tbilisi, Georgia: Mirani Publishing House

Eliade, M. (1964) *Myth and Reality*, London: George Allen & Unwin

Eliade, M. (1981) *Tales of the Sacred and the Supernatural*, Philadelphia: The Westminster Press.

Eliade, M. (2003) *Rites and Symbols of Initiation*, Putnam, Connecticut: Spring Publications (originally published by Harper Bros., New York, 1958).

Joshua Project http://www.joshuaproject.net/peopctry.php?rop3= 100079&rog3=RS [accessed 13/11/09]).

Kremer, J.W. (1988) 'Shamanic Tales as Ways of Personal Empowerment.' In Gary Doore (ed.) *Shaman's Path: Healing, Personal Growth and Empowerment*, Boston, Massachusetts: Shambhala Publications. Pp.189-199.

Lévi-Strauss, C. (1968) *Structural Anthropology*, Harmondsworth: Penguin.

Turner, V. (1982) *From Ritual to Theatre: The Human Seriousness of Play*, New York: PAJ Publications (A division of Performing Arts Journal, Inc.).

Turner, V. (1985) *On the Edge of the Bush: Anthropology as Experience.* Tucson, AZ: University of Arizona Press.

Winterbourne, A. (2007) *When The Norns Have Spoken: Time and Fate in Germanic Paganism*, Wales: Superscript.

Shamanism: Countable or Uncountable?
Mircea Eliade Revisited

Writing about shamanism has always been problematic as "the subject area resists 'objective' analysis and is sufficiently beyond mainstream research to foil ...writing about it in a conventional academic way" (Wallis, 2003, p.13). Though what follows is an example of insider research, every effort has been made to ensure that the findings "express the level of insight and constructive, critical evaluation which one's academic peers require for acceptable scholarship" (Wallis, 2003, p.6). However, we have to accept that despite our best efforts it is highly unlikely we can ever be truly objective, and this applies to both academics and practitioners alike.

The practice of shamanism is understood to encompass a personalistic view of the world, in which life is seen to be not only about beliefs and practices, but also about relationships–how we are related, and how we relate to each other. In shamanism the notion of interdependence "is the idea of the kinship of all life, the recognition that nothing can exist in and of itself without being in relationship to other things, and therefore that it is insane for us to consider ourselves as essentially unrelated parts of the whole Earth" (Halifax in Nicholson, (comp.), 1987, p.220). And through neurotheology, this assertion so often heard expressed in neo-shamanic circles that all life is connected, can now be substantiated. This is because

it has been shown that during mystical ecstasy (or its equivalent, entheogenic shamanic states [states induced by ingesting hallucinogens]), the individual experiences a blurring of the boundaries on the ego and feels at "one with Nature"; the ego is no longer confined within the body, but extends outward to all of Nature; other living beings come to share in the ego, as an authentic communion with the total environment, which is sensed as in some way divine (Ruck, Staples, et al., 2007, p.76).

Further justification for the belief that all life is connected can be found in the fact that the elementary particles that make up all matter, by their gravitational, electromagnetic or nuclear field, are coextensive with the whole universe, and as man is composed of these particles, he is thus in union with the entire cosmos (see Eliade, pp.285-286). Whether he wants to be or not is immaterial.

Traditionally it was the role of the shaman to maintain the equilibrium of the community he / she represented by focussing on the interrelationships within it and resolving any discord there may have been. The neo-shaman, on the other hand, tends to work within in a much wider community where not everyone shares the same practices and beliefs. Consequently, his or her work is generally more concerned with helping individuals rather than the community.

In contrast to indigenous shamanisms, there is little community or even an after-shamanic-experience forum for core-shamanism practitioners. Indeed, many I have met complain that there is no 'after-workshop' opportunity for communal interaction. Harnerists essentially teach the practice, then you are on your own. Only the more seasoned and dedicated practitioners go on to form drumming groups where practitioners come together to journey (for oneself or each other) and share experiences (Wallis, 2003, p.61).

The following observation by the Hungarian academic Vilmos Voigt is also intended to draw attention to the limitations of neo-shamanism: "None of the actual personal or social problems of the unemployed or the bored rich are solved by attending urban drum classes" (Voigt, 2009, p.216). On the other hand, it is doubtful whether it could be said that attending services held in any churches, temples, mosques or synagogues can satisfactorily solve the above-mentioned problems either. What such practices can be said to do, though, is to help us to make some sense out of our existence and also to make our lives more manageable.

In the 1960s neo-shamanism became one of the Western spiritualities that capitalized on the Eliadean vision presented in his seminal work *Shamanism: Archaic Techniques of Esctasy*, which was an attempt "to descend to the depth of the human spiritual tradition, to find the roots of the primal religion and to decipher its universal archaic patterns that could be retrieved for future spiritual regeneration" (Znamenski, 2009, pp.187-188). According to Eliade, what "archaic" peoples could do and what modern ones were unable to do was, through myth and ritual, to return to the primal time, and the most accessible way to do so was through fiction. "Eliade was convinced that in contemporary society literature was one of the remaining strongholds of ancient mythological conscience; he called fiction "the residue of mythological behaviour" in modern world" (Znamenski, 2009, p. 189), and the fiction he himself wrote reflected this (see Berman, 2008, pp.213-246).

Eliade's scholarship appealed, in particular, "to American and European spiritual seekers who revolted against Western civilisation and who felt at home with all his eclectic cross-cultural symbolism" (Znamenski, 2009, p. 196).

Despite the fact that Eliade's reputation has become somewhat tarnished in recent years[2], his importance in the history of the development of neo-shamanism cannot be over-emphasized. For in addition to rehabilitating nature religions in the eyes of Westerners, he stretched out the geographic borders of shamanism so that it came to be applied to "all non-Western and pre-Christian European spiritualities which did not fit the format of organised world religions and in which spiritual practitioners worked in altered states" (Znamenski, 2009, p.197).

One of the criticisms levelled against Eliade is for the dubious nature of his research, which was often based on second-hand accounts. If he were here with us today, however, he would no doubt dispute this accusation for, as he states in one of his journals, "I have always made an effort to draw the *facts* and their interpretation from those who still participate in a pre-Christian religious universe" (Eliade, 1977, p.101). It should also be remembered that as a historian of religions, field work was never part of his remit

Although it is true that Eliade himself did no original research, *Shamanism: Archaic Techniques of Esctasy* was a break-through in that it provided a broad overview of what was known about shamanism at the time, and anthropologists then built on what he had instigated by actually going out to work in the field and live among shamans in order to learn more about them. For example, a researcher who became a participant in the 1950s was Francis Huxley, a British anthropologist who lived with Urubu and Tembe people in the Brazilian Amazon. In *Affable Savages: An Anthropologist among the Urubu Indians of Brazil*, published in 1956, Huxley described how he participated in a healing ceremony and tried some of the strong tobacco that the shamans smoked. Direct experiences like this helped to change anthropo-logical thinking, since now they were better able to see the world as the people they studied did.

One of the people profoundly influenced by Eliade's schol-arship was the American anthropologist Michael Harner, who then went on to develop "core shamanism" by singling out what he viewed as common archetypes of shamanism from all over the world. And out of this he developed what he refers to as Core Shamanic Counselling, a form of counselling designed to enable clients to become their own shamans – in other words, to teach them how to journey to their power animals and sacred teachers in non-ordinary reality to find answers to their problems for themselves. Training courses are run by organizations such as the Foundation for Shamanic Studies, established by Harner himself, and the Scandinavian Centre for Shamanic Studies run by Jonathan Horwitz. So without Eliade there might have been no Michael Harner, and `without Harner's *The Way of the Shaman* and the books of Carlos Castaneda (whose doctoral thesis was actually examined by Harner), the interest currently being shown in shamanism would surely never have developed in the way that it has.

As for what attracted Eliade (who referred to himself as Christian) to shamanism, his interest was very much influenced by traditionalism.

Traditionalism was a loose movement that spread in the turbulent European atmosphere of the 1920s and the 1930s. Grounded in Romanticism and linked to European esotericism, it united conservative European ideologists, writers, and spiritual seekers who crusaded against the legacy of Western civilization, particularly Enlightenment, capitalism and materialism. Overwhelmed by modernity, these people were seeking to solace themselves in their own indigenous roots and soil. The quest for roots meant the retrieval of ideal ancient indigenous spirituality that, as they argued, was erased by cosmopolitan Judeo-Christian tradition (Znamenski, 2009, p184).

One of their leading proponents was Julius Evola, who conveyed the intellectual stance of this movement in his book *Revolt against the Modern World.*

Eliade believed that the sacred should be discussed on its own terms without being reduced to social life, history, economics, and brain function, and his method became known as the phenomenological approach. As he pointed out in his own diary in 1946, his intention was to present shamanism in the general perspective of the history of religions rather than as an aberrant phenomenon belonging more to psychiatry" (see Eliade, 1990, p.18).

One of Eliade's concerns was that in his efforts to give himself the means of knowing the world objectively and mastering it, modern western man was in danger of emptying the world of all its extranatural meaning (see Eliade, 1977, p.55). "The neuropath loses the sense of reality. He can no longer grasp a reality that is of construction, a mask. The neuropath demystifies life, culture, the spiritual life. Not that the neurosis puts more perfect instruments of knowledge at his disposal than those of the normal man – but because the neurotic can no longer grasp the deep meaning of things, and consequently, he can no longer believe in their *reality*" (Eliade, 1977, p.144).

Though he is surely to be respected for not attempting to remove the "magic" from shamanism by trying to explain away exactly what it is that shamans do when they journey into non-ordinary reality, his cross-cultural and universal vision of shamanism is not so acceptable to the present-day postmodernist thinkers who treat "with suspicion any grand comparison-the method Eliade used in his numerous books and articles" (Znamenski, 2009, p.200). However, it seems to me that by referring to "shamanisms" rather than "shamanism" as Jane Monnig Atkinson (1992) and Robert J. Wallis (2003) do, the importance of shamanism becomes trivialized, and thus this approach does its practitioners more harm than good.

There was a time, following on from Eliade, when the collective aspect of shamanism was emphasized, with it being seen "as a cosmological system in which shamans play specific roles, depending upon the cultural and historical context" (Langdon 1991a, b), and anthropology's task was to document the different varieties. In the field of neo-shamanism, however, a case is made for having shamanism without shamans (Brunelli 1996) and the emphasis is placed the persistence of collective visions without practicing shamans ... In the same way that New Agers appropriate shamanic practices, native shamans show themselves equally able to appropriate a variety of different cultural traditions, including those of biomedicine (Greene 1998; Dobkin del Rios 1992; Luna and Amaringo 1991), and shamans intermingle with hegemonic images of native magical powers to become part of the network of hybrid healing and sorcery alternatives outside Indian communities (Joralemon 1986; Pinzón and Ramírez 1992; Taussig 1987; Vidal 2002; Vidal and Whitehead 2002). (Langdon, 2006, p.28).

On the basis of this, Langdon then goes on to argue that

an adequate understanding of shamanism, like other social phenomenon, must abandon the concept that culture is a holistic unity with clear boundaries and space. Also, our monographs must drop the monophonic authorial voice, in favor of portraying the multiplicity of shamanic phenomena, where there is less unity, more fragmentation and no clear boundaries (Gupta and Ferguson 2001: 5). (Langdon, 2006, p.29).

The important point that is being made here is that this applies to other social phenomenon too, not only shamanism. Following on from this, if we are going to refer to shamanisms, then we need to refer to christianities, buddhisms, etc., too. Atkinson is another who makes out a case for referring to shamanisms rather than shamanism,

The article "Shamanisms Today," by J.M. Atkinson (1992), appeared in the *Annual Review of Anthropology*. Atkinson states that "Just a few decades ago, shamanism appeared to be a dead issue in American anthropology" (p.307). Atkinson cites Taussig, who writes that "shamanism is ... a made-up,

Modern Western category, and artful reification of disparate practices, snatches of folklore and overarching folkloriza-tions, residues of long-established myths intermingled with the politics of academic departments, curricula, conferences, journal juries [and] funding agencies" (Atkinson, 1992, p.307). In spite of Taussig's criticism of the subject, Atkinson presents a scholarly account of this subject. She concurs with Holmberg's (1983) observation that there is really no single unified shamanism per se but that there exists a plurality of *shamanisms*, each with its own individual variations (Noblitt & Perskins, 2000, p.106).

However, if we consider all the different cultures in which it is practised, it is only to be expected that there is variation rather than uniformity so why the need to refer to any religion in the plural? Does it serve any useful purpose and, if not, then why bother to use it?

If there is considered to be no need to turn the names of other religions into countable nouns, then there is no reason to do so with shamanism either, at least for those of us who regard it as a religion. After all, there is not one religion that does not take a variety of different forms, so why single out shamanism for such grammatical treatment?

Moreover, even if it is agreed that there are a variety of shamanisms, it has in any case become more or less impossible to differentiate between those that are indigenous and those which are neo-shamanic due to the way in which the two now cross over and influence each other. Michael Harmer and other core-shamanists, for example, are now teaching their techniques to the Sami and Inuit (see Wallis, 2003, p.31). Given that indigenous and neo-shamanism can thus no longer be considered to be distinct and separate from each other, there would seem to be little point in regarding them as countable, which is why the uncountable form of the noun is, in my view, to be preferred.

And instead of referring to shamanisms with a small s, it makes more sense to refer to forms of Shamanism, using the uncountable noun with a capital S, as capitalisation locates, rather than downsizes Shamanism alongside universally recognised religions such as Christianity. Wallis suggests 'pluralising, cumbersome though it may be, embraces diversity and difference, rather than generalities' (Wallis, 2003, p.30). However, by referring instead to forms of shamanism exactly the same effect can be achieved so the point he makes is invalid.

Actually, there is no need for me to defend Eliade's position, which is that we have the right to generalise in the history of religions, as he can stand up for himself:

Socrates tried to learn the essence of virtue. Examples of different virtues didn't satisfy him – he asked his interlocutors for a definition of virtue. He forced them to observe that the multiplicity of virtues doesn't mean that there doesn't exist an element that is common to all. (I think of my controversies with the historicists, who refuse to accept structures and believe only in the "concrete," isolated and defined by its own historico-cultural context (Eliade, 1977, p.151).

Eliade does, however, add the proviso that we should only do so "On the condition that we present the essential on the scale on which we are working, and that we be coherent" (Eliade, 1977, p.202).

As for Eliade's literary output, it is relatively unknown compared to his other work. However, as we shall now see, it was a great deal more than just a mere sideline. Thus no re-evaluation of his importance could be regarded as complete without considering it, especially as he wrote what can be regarded as the first shamanic novel, *The Forbidden Forest*, which was translated into English in the late 1970s. This pre-dated Castaneda's efforts and all the novelists who post-dated him such as Lynn Andrews and

Mary Summer Rain's books about her blind teacher "No- Eyes".

So not only did Eliade write about shamanism and inspire others to do so, but he also wrote what can be described as shamanic stories himself. A shamanic story is understood here to be one that is either based on or inspired by a shamanic journey (a numinous experience in non-ordinary reality) or one that contains a number of the elements typical of such a journey. Characteristics typical of the genre include the way in which the stories all tend to contain embedded texts (often the account of the shamanic journey itself), how the number of actors is clearly limited as one would expect in subjective accounts of what can be regarded as inner journeys, and how they have the potential to provide a medium through which psychic states that might otherwise be difficult to put into words can be expressed. And the short story that will be considered here, *A Great Man* (*Un om mare* in Romanian), is very much typical of the genre, being a story about soul loss through giving power away.

In his Foreword to *Tales of the Sacred and the Supernatural*, Eliade admits to repeatedly taking up "the themes of *sortie du temps*, or temporal dislocation, and of the alteration or the trans-mutation of space" (Eliade, 1981, p.10), and the result very much reflects what shamans claim to experience in their accounts of their journeys into non-ordinary reality, adding further support to the case being made for regarding certain of Eliade's stories as shamanic.

One of the reasons for the incipient success of Eliade as a writer of fiction could ironically be his world fame as a scholar of myth and religion, with the general consensus of opinion being that a scholar's literary efforts are just a sideline (see Calinescu, 1978, p.381). However, if his fictional writing were nothing more than a sideline for Eliade, it is unlikely he would have written the ten novels, twenty-five novellas and short stories, and two complete plays that he did (see Ricketts, 1982, pp.364-365), and it has even been suggested that Eliade's literary work could "prove, in the long run, to be of more enduring value than many of his scholarly writings" (Ricketts, 2001, p.93).

Eliade does not use the term "shamanic story" himself in any of his work to describe the kind of tale he writes. In fact, he "never exactly, explicitly defined the nature of his fantastic style" (Simion, 2001, p.153). However, Eliade scholars Matei Calinescu and Walter Strauss have classified it as a form of "magic realism". "It is a style he has developed by himself, which owes something to the Romanian folktale and something to his vast reading in mythology and literature" (Rickets, 2006, p.373). It is a style of storytelling in which "the point of departure is 'realistic' (recognizable events in chronological succession, everyday atmosphere, verisimilitude, characters with more or less predictable psychological reactions), but soon strange discontinuities or gaps appear in the 'normal,' true-to-life texture of the narrative" (Calinescu, 1978, p.386). Eliade himself describes the technique he employs as "the imperfectly gradual transmutation of a commonplace setting into a new 'world' without, however, losing the proper, everyday, or 'natural' structure and qualities of that setting" (Eliade, 1981, pp.10-11). In the case of *A Great Man*, written in 1945, the anomaly is the unnatural and unstoppable physical growth of the main character, which the author then sets out to explore.

Eliade uses the particular style of writing found in fantastic literature in a rather different way to other writers:

Traditionally, fantastic literature has derived its effects from a sense of menace posed by the sudden interruption of the incomprehensible (the supernatural) in the comprehensible flow of ordinary life. Everyday reality is seen as reassuring and the obscure world of the supernatural ... is conceived of as dangerous, malevolent and destructive. With Eliade this relation is reversed: it is everyday reality which is essentially incomprehensible, meaningless and cruel. It is only when we recognize the presence of the other world (miracle, primordial time) that we are saved from meaningless (Calinescu, 1982, p.150).

In the case of *A Great Man,* for example, it is everyday reality that becomes dangerous, malevolent and destructive as far as Cucoaneş is concerned, and it is only when he escapes from it that he seems to find any chance of some kind of salvation.

The story starts with the narrator meeting up with, by chance, an acquaintance from his grammar school days, Eugen Cucoaneş, who comes to him with an unusual problem. He discovers he has suddenly started to grow again physically at a rapid rate and the doctors can offer him no solution. However, is it that he really grows in physical stature or is it that everyone is so intent on giving their power away that they build him up into someone he is not and never will be? Is what happens perhaps in part due to Eugen's own inflated ego too? Either way, things develop at an alarming pace and he finds himself unable to cope with the consequences, all the attention he receives for example, and so escapes from the gaze of the curious, with the narrator's help, into the forests of the Transylvanian Alps. One is reminded somehow of the tragic story of Greta Garbo, who just wanted to be left alone at the end of her days–her story being a parallel to this in many ways, or even the reclusive Michael Jackson.

Eugen Cucoaneş is described at one point as having "the air of a prophet of apocalyptic horror"–the kind of monster the media create to satisfy our lust for such larger than life personages.

The medical diagnosis of Cucoaneş' condition–macranthropy, information on the diet he is advised to follow and on the vitamins and minerals he is supposed to avoid, provide the verisimilitude referred to earlier and also help to make the unusual nature of what follows during the course of the narrative more plausible, as of course do the precise measurements taken of Cucoaneş' increase in height.

At another point the narrator remarks "One expected to see him raising Neptune's trident or hurling thunderbolts like

Jupiter–and all that would have ensued would not have surprised you more than his personal appearance. His beard had grown prodigiously in those last four days, completely changing his face and turning it into a theophany" (Eliade & Niculescu, 1990, p.65). In other words, depending on the way you choose to interpret the tale, Eugen takes on the appearance of, or is built up into, a godlike figure. In fact the narrator is so taken in by the transformation that he more than half expects Eugen to be able to answer the unanswerable: "Tell us whether God exists and what we ought to do that we too may know him. Tell us whether life continues after death and how we are to prepare for it. *Tell us something!* Teach us!" (Eliade & Niculescu, 1990, p.69). At the end of the tale, however, Eugen disappears without a trace and is never heard of again, rather like the rise and fall of some of the popular iconic figures, footballers and rock stars, who appear in the media, or the false gods that some of us make the mistake of bowing down to due to our own lack of self-belief.

It has to be admitted that the interpretation of the tale proposed here is very much a personal one, and not one Eliade would have necessarily agreed with. Writing about his own fictional work, he makes the point that "the 'fantastic' elements disclose–or, more precisely, create–a series of 'parallel worlds' which do not pretend to be 'symbols' of something else" (Eliade, 1981, p.12). Be that as it may, the fact of the matter is that they are still open to interpretation as such by the reader, and the writer has little control over this. In the same way, for that matter, teachers can neverbe sure that what they teach will necessarily be understood in the way they had intended it to be.

When we are told that the valleys resounded to Cucoaneş' words, and that it was "like the forewarnings of a storm; the trees trembled and the branches bent", we are reminded of God talking to Moses on Mount Sinai, and then we have the revealing words "we all made ourselves, it seemed, smaller than we thought we were." It could be argued that what we have here is a glimmer of self-realization as the narrator has a vague awareness of the fact that he might actually have been partly responsible forCucoaneş' transformation into a larger-than-life figure.

The question as to why Cucoaneş, a non-smoker, takes up the habit in the course of the story once his transformation starts to take place is an interesting one. The use of hallucinogenic drugs or alcoholic is not uncommon for ritual purposes or for entering trancelike states in certain communities and this could well be the reason why Eliade chose to introduce smoking into the tale, either unconsciously or perhaps even to point out the parallels between the journey of Cucoaneş and that of a shaman. Further into the narrative, Cucoaneş' speech becomes indecipherable, as if he is talking in tongues, another indication of being in a trancelike state, a state of non-ordinary reality, as is the inability to hear what is taking place in this reality as Cucoaneş eventually seems unable to do. Cucoaneş also talks about hearing strange things: "I seem to hear the ticking all the time, but it's not exactly a clock, it seems to be *something else*, which beats in everything at the same time" (Eliade & Niculescu, 1990, p.47). It is as if he is experiencing some form of heightened awareness, as if he can perceive life in everything and as if he can perceive how all life is connected in some way–very much what a shaman is said to experience. Consequently, we have to conclude that the parallels are more than just coincidental, especially if we take into account too what we know about Eliade's detailed knowledge of shamanism.

The argument has been put forward that we have to redis-cover myths because it is only thanks to them that man can redis-cover the "sacramental dimension of existence" (see Simion, 2001, p.146), which is perhaps why Eliade in his stories can be seen to either search for, or even attempt to recreate, the sacred out of the profane. The godlike figure that Eugen Cucoaneş becomes transformed into during the course of this particular tale provides a good example of this.

For Eliade there is a continuity between myth and literary fiction because they both recount the creation of a universe parallel to the everyday world. He also saw myth as having an exemplary value in primitive societies and believed that this could also be applied to literary works (see Eliade, 1981, p.12). Indeed, he once described literature as the daughter of mythology because not only does it inherit its function of telling adventures, but also its function of telling what significantly happened in the world (see Simion, 2001, p.159). As *A Great Man* shows, his own fictional writing was clearly intended to fulfil both these functions.

Eliade talks about his literary work and the relationship between myth and literary fiction in *Ordeal by Labyrinth* (1982), a collection of conversations he had with Claude-Henri Rocquet: I believe that all narration, even that of a very ordinary event, is an extension of the stories told by the great myths that explain how this world came into being and how our condition has come to be as we know it today. I think that an interest in narration is part of our mode of being in the world. It answers an essential need to hear what has happened, what men have done, what they have the power to do (Eliade, 1982, p.166). And our interest in narrative, as accounted for by Eliade, brings to mind the Navajo saying: "We shall exist as long as our stories are moist with our breath."

Let us now turn our attention to another one of Eliade's shamanic stories:

"With the Gypsy Girls" ... abounds in symbols drawn from mythology and the history of religions–such as the labyrinth, the carriage driver as Charon, etc.–but deciphering them does not exhaust the meaning Eliade wishes the reader to derive from the story. The "revelation" as Eliade calls it comes from the total impact of the story, conveyed not *rationally*, but *intuitively* ... just as myths make their impact on believers. Eliade would make us "believe" in the world he creates in his stories and, entering into them, be "awakened" and enlightened (Ricketts, 1982, pp.372-373).

In this sense, the story is very much an example of what Jürgen Kremer defines as "tales of power"–conscious verbal constructions based on numinous experiences in non-ordinary reality, "which guide individuals and help them to integrate the spiritual, mythical, or archetypal aspects of their internal and external experience in unique, meaningful, and fulfilling ways" (Kremer, 1988, p.192). This is in fact a characteristic shared by all shamanic stories.

Many of Eliade's literary works can be classified in the genre of fantastic literature. This is true, for example, of "With the Gypsy Girls" ... The story, like all of Eliade's fiction, is set in an *apparently* realistic world, in this case the Bucharest of the 1930s. The hero, Gavrilescu, enters a kind of bordello operated by Gypsies and stays, he thinks, a few hours. When he emerges, some twelve years have elapsed. The passage from one time rhythm or zone to another is a favorite device, of course, of writers of fantasy, and Eliade has used it a number of times. But Eliade states in his *Journal,* that even the "real world" of the first and last parts of "Gypsy Girls" is to be taken as a "mythical geography"–which would mean that the reader enters into a "fantasy world" as soon as he begins to read, a world in which the hero's fantastic adventure is not "unreal" (Ricketts, 1982, p.373).

Let us now consider the plot of the story in more detail. Gavrilescu, a 49-year-old piano teacher, has to get off the tram he is travelling on because he realises he has left his briefcase with his music behind. He gets off, by chance, outside the house of the notorious gypsies, which he enters and never really returns from again.

Gradually we come to realise that Gavrilescu has in fact set off unawares on a journey into another reality. We learn, for example, that he followed the girl who enticed him into the house as if he were 'bewitched' and the madam of the brothel informs him that all the clocks have stopped again. In other words, he stepped out of historical time the moment he crossed the threshold. We then learn that "He entered stepping on the carpet which became even thicker and softer; it seemed as if he were walking on mattresses" (Eliade, 1992, p.187). The feeling of walking on something that lacks solidity is not atypical in accounts of shamanic journeys, particularly in those to the Upper World. However, this particular journey, as we gradually discover, turns out to be to the Land of the Dead. Gavrilescu's memory then starts to play tricks with him when he attempts to reminisce about the past: "Something terrible happened," he continued. "But what? What on earth could have happened? Strange, I cannot remember" (Eliade, 1992, p.190). After that, he is led into a dance, rather like the whirling dervishes perform to enter trancelike states: "The girl whirled him in a reel, shouting and whistling ... after a time he gave up resisting and was no longer conscious of anything ... Gavrilescu felt the room swaying around him, and once more he put his hand to his head. 'For God's sake, what have you done to me?' " (Eliade, 1992, pp.191 & 192).

The story is also about how we walk around with our eyes closed, unaware of all the hidden possibilities available to us: "For so many years he had ridden past this garden, never once moved by curiosity to get off the tram and consider it closely" (Eliade, 1992, p.185).

Gavrilescu then find himself naked for some reason and tries to cover himself with the only thing close at hand–a curtain: "The curtain curling around me like a winding sheet ... That curtain was a real winding sheet, I tell you. It was skin-tight. It was wound around and so tight that I couldn't breathe. And such heat ... it's a wonder that I'm still alive" (Eliade, 1992, p.203). It is here that the association with death is really brought home to the reader.

To cut a long story short, when Gavrilescu eventually manages to back home, he finds his key no longer fits his lock and his wife Elsa no longer living there. He then learns from the owner of a nearby pub that when Elsa's husband went missing twelve years previously she had made the decision to return to her family in Germany

At a loss as to what to do, the bemused Gavrilescu returns to the house of the gypsies, where he enters the room of a German prostitute he has paid for only to find his long lost love Hildegard waiting for him, someone we are led to believe had died many years before, who urges Gavrilescu to leave the house with her. They get into a cab together, the driver asks Hildegard where to go, and this is her answer: "Drive us to the woods, and go the longest way," said the girl. "And drive slowly. We're in no hurry." Thus the reader understands the two lovers are being taken to the Land of the Dead and that the cab driver is none other than Charon (see Calinescu, 1982, p.152). And this is how the tale ends:

"Hildegard," he began finally. "Something's happening to me, and I don't quite understand what. If I hadn't heard you speak to the cab driver, I would think I was dreaming." The girl turned her head toward him and smiled. "We're all dreaming," she said. "That's how it begins. As if in a dream ..."

Let us hope that someone finally gets round to making a screenplay out of *With the Gypsies* and an enterprising producer takes on the project as what a great final scene to a film this would make! This English translation of the story can be found in the collection *Mystic Tales: The Sacred and the Profane*. It has been outlined here to show *A Great Man* is not a "one-off" and that Eliade wrote other examples of shamanic stories too.

In conclusion, for the influence he has had on all those who have followed him, apart from all the other reasons that have been pointed out in this chapter, the time has surely come to reassess Eliade's importance and to restore him to his rightful place at the head of the table instead of failing to even give him a mention, which is unfortunately what seems to have been the recent trend.

References

Atkinson, Jane Monnig (1992) 'Shamanisms Today.' In Annual Review of Anthropology 21: pp.307-330.

Berman, M. (2007) *The Nature of Shamanism and the Shamanic Story*, Newcastle: Cambridge Scholars Publishing.

Berman, M (2008) *Soul Loss and the Shamanic Story*, Newcastle: Cambridge scholars Publishing.

Brunelli, G. (1996) "Do Xamanismo aos Xamãs: estratégias Tupi-Mondé frente à sociedade envolvente". In: E.J.M. Langdon, (org.), *Xamanismo no Brasil: Novas Perspectivas*. Florianópolis: Editora UFSC. pp. 233-266.

Calinescu, M. (1978) 'The Disguises of Miracle: Notes on Mircea Eliade's Fiction.' In Bryan Rennie (ed.) (2006) *Mircea Eliade: A Critical Reader*, London: Equinox Publishing Ltd.

Calinescu, M. (1982) 'The Function of the Unreal: Reflections on Mircea Eliade's Short Fiction.' In Norman J. Girardot and Max Linscott

Dobkin de Rios, M. (1992) *Amazon Healer: The Life and Times of an Urban Shaman*. Bridport, U.K.: Prison Press. Dist. by Avery Pub.

Eliade, M. (1957) *The Sacred and the Profane: The Nature of Religion*, New York: Harper & Row.

Eliade, M. (1960) *Myths, Dreams and Mysteries*, New York: Harper & Row.

Eliade, M. (1964) *Myth and Reality*, London: George Allen & Unwin

Eliade, Mircea (1964) *Shamanism: Archaic Techniques of Esctasy*, Princeton, NJ: Princeton University Press (originally published in French in 1951).

Eliade, M. (1965) *The Myth of the Eternal Return*, New York: Harper (originally published in 1949).

Eliade, M. (1967) *From Primitives to Zen: A Thematic Sourcebook of the History of Religions*, London: Collins.

Eliade, M. (1969) *The Quest: History and Meaning in Religion*, London: University of Chicago Press.

Eliade, M. (1981) *Tales of the Sacred and the Supernatural*, Philadelphia: The Westminster Press.

Eliade, M. (1982) *Ordeal by Labyrinth: Conversations with Claude-Henri Rocquet*, Chicago: University of Chicago Press.

Eliade, M. (1989) *Shamanism: Archaic techniques of ecstasy*, London: Arkana (first published in the USA by Pantheon Books 1964).

Eliade, M. & Niculescu, M. (1990) *Fantastic Tales*, London: Forest Books.

Eliade, M. (1991) *Images and Symbols*, New Jersey: Princeton University Press (The original edition is copyright Librairie Gallimard 1952).

Eliade, M. (1992) Mystic Stories: *The Sacred and the Profane*, New York: Columbia University Press.

Eliade, M. (2003) *Rites and Symbols of Initiation*, Putnam, Connecticut: Spring Publications (originally published by Harper Bros., New York, 1958).

Eliade, M. (2006) 'Folklorul ca instrument de cunoastere,' *Revista Fundatilor Regale*, IV, 4 (April 19, 1937). In Bryan Rennie (ed.) *Mircea Eliade: A Critical Reader*, London: Equinox Publishing Ltd.

Eliade, M. (1977) *No Souvenirs: Journal 1957-1969*, San Francisco: Harper & Row Publishers (originally published in France as *Fragments d'un journal* in 1973).

Eliade, Mircea (1990) *Autobiography*, Chicago: University of Chicago Press.

Greene, S. (1998) "The Shaman's Needle: Development,

Shamanic Agency, and Intermedicality in Aguaruna Lands, Peru". *American Ethnologist*, 25(4): 634-658.

Halifax, J. (1987) "Shamanism, Mind, and No Self" in Nicholson, S. (comp.) *Shamanism: An Expanded View of Reality*, Wheaton: The Theosophical Publishing House.

Hamayon, R. (2000) '"Ecstasy" and the Self or the West-dreamt Shamanism: From Socrates to New Age Postmodernism,' (The draft of a paper given at the University of Hong Kong, not intended for publication).

Harner, M. (1990 3rd Edition) *The Way of the Shaman*, Harper & Row (first published by Harper & Row in 1980).

Joralemon, D. (1986) "The Performing Patient in Ritual Healing". *Social Science and Medicine*. 23(9): 841-85.

Langdon, E. J. (1991a) "Poder y Autoridad en el proceso político siona: desarrollo y muerte del shaman". In: J. Ehrenreich, (org.), *Antropologia Política en el Ecuador*. Quito: Ediciones ABYA-YALA. pp. 161-188.

Langdon, E. J. (1991b) "Interethnic Processes Affecting the Survival of Shamans: A Comparative Analysis". In: C. E. Pinzón and R. Suárez P. (orgs), *La Otra America en Construcción: Medicinas Tradicionales, Religiones Populares*. Bogotá: Instituto Colombiano de Antropología e Instituto Colombiano de Cultura. pp. 44-65.

Langdon, E. J. (2006) Shamans and Shamanisms: 'Reflections on Anthropological Dilemmas of Modernity.' In vibrant v.4 n.2 p. 27-48 www.vibrant.org.br/downloads/v4n2_langdon.htm [accessed 18/09/09].

Luna, L. E. & Amaringo, P. (1991) *Ayahuasca Visions. The Religious Imaginery of Pablo Amaringo*. Berkeley: North Atlantic Books.

Noblitt, J.R. & Perskin, P.S. (2000) Cult and Ritual Abuse: Its History, Anthropology, and Recent Discovery in Cntempoarary America Westport, CT Praeger Publications.

Rennie, B. S. (1996) *Reconstructing Eliade: making sense of religion*, Albany: State University of New York Press.

Rennie, B. (ed.) (2001) *Changing Religious Worlds: The Meaning and End of Mircea Eliade*, New York: State University of New York Press.

Rennie, B. (ed.) (2006) *Mircea Eliade: A Critical Reader*, London: Equinox Publishing Ltd.

Ricketts, M.L. (1982) 'On Reading Eliade's Stories as Myths for Moderns.' In Bryan Rennie (ed.) (2006) *Mircea Eliade: A Critical Reader*, London: Equinox Publishing Ltd.

Ricketts, M.L. & Girardot, N.J. (eds.) (1982) *Imagination and Meaning: The Scholarly and Literary Worlds of Mircea Eliade*, New York: The Seabury Press.

Rickets, M.L. (2001) 'The United States Response to Mircea Eliade's Fiction.' In Bryan Rennie (ed.) *Changing Religious Worlds: The Meaning and End of Mircea Eliade*, New York: State University of New York Press.

Ruck, Carl A.P., Staples, B.D., Celdran J.A.G., Hoffman, M.A. (2007) *The Hidden World: Survival of Pagan Shamanic Themes in European Fairytales*, North Carolina: Carolina Academic Press.

Simion, E. (2001) *Mircea Eliade: A spirit of Amplitude*, New York: Columbia University Press.

Taussig, M. (1987) *Shamanism, Colonialism, and the Wild Man: A Study in Terror and Healing.* Chicago: University of Chicago Press.

Vidal, S. M. & Whitehead N. L. (2002) "Dark Shamans and the Shamanic State: Sorcery and Witchcraft as Political Process in Guyana and the Venezuelan Amazon". In: N. Whitehead and R. Wright, (ed.), *In Darkness and Secrecy: The Anthropology of Assault Sorcery and Witchcraft in Amazonia.* Durham: Duke University Press. pp. 51-80.

Vidal, S. M. (2002) "El Chamanismo de los Arawakos del Rio Negro: Su Influencia en la Política Local y Regional en el Amazonas de Venezuela". *Série Antropologia.* Brasília: UNB. No. 313.

Voigt, V. (2009) Book Review of Andrei Znamenski's *The Beauty of the Primitive*. In SHAMAN Vol 17 Numbers 1 and 2, Budapest: Molnar & Kelemen Oriental Publishers.

Wallis, Robert J. (2003) *Shamans/Neo-Shamans: Ecstasy, Alternative Archaeologies and Contemporary Pagans*, London: Routledge.

Znamenski, Andrei. (2009) 'Quest for Primal Knowledge: Mircea Eliade, Traditionalism, and "Archaic Techniques of Ecstasy"' In SHAMAN Vol. 17 Numbers 1 and 2, Budapest: Molnar & Kelemen Oriental Publishers.

The Goddess of Mount Daimugenzan and the Perpetual Life-giving Wine

In the story that follows Mount Daimugenzan represents the axis mundi, where the tennin can be found, and the Mountain Goddess acts as Okureha's Spirit Helper on the journey she undertakes. Tennin are heavenly beings, a group that also includes the tennyo - who are celestial maidens. In artwork, they appear most frequently as dancers and musicians who adorn Buddhist statuary, paintings, and temple structures in China, Japan and Southeast Asia. Their attributes are not clearly specified in Buddhist texts, and thus their appearance is quite varied. In Japan, they are often shown standing or sitting on clouds or flying through the air in graceful poses, playing musical instruments, or scattering flowers to give praise to the gods.

The Perpetual Life-giving Wine

Between the north-eastern boundary of Totomi Province and the north-western of Suruga Province stands a lofty mountain, Daimugenzan. It is a wild and rugged mountain, clad nearly three-quarters up with lofty pines, *yenoki*, *icho*, camphors, etc. There are but few paths, and hardly any one goes up the hill. About halfway up through the forest is a shrine erected to Kwannon; but it is so small that no priest lives there, and the building is rotting away. No one knows why it was put up in such an inaccessible place—except, perhaps, one solitary girl and her parents, who used to go there for some reason of their own.

One day, about 1107 A.D., the girl was praying for her mother's recovery from sickness. Okureha was her name. She lived at Tashiro, at the foot of the mountain, and was the beauty of the countryside,—the daughter of a much-loved samurai of some importance. Amid the solemn silence Okureha clapped her hands thrice before Kwannon as she prayed, causing mountain echoes to resound. Having finished her prayers, Okureha began to make her way downwards, when she was suddenly sprung upon by a ruffianly-looking man, who seized her by the arm.

She cried aloud for help; but nothing came except the echoes of her voice, and she gave herself up for lost.

Suddenly a piercing cold breeze came along, carrying the autumn leaves in little columns. Okureha struggled violently with her assailant, who seemed to weaken to the cold wind as it struck his face. Okureha weakened too. In a few seconds the man fell down as in a drunken sleep, and she was on the point of falling (she knew not why) and of sleeping (scarce could she keep her eyes open). Just then the wind came hot instead of cold, and she felt herself awake again. On looking up she saw advancing towards her a beautiful girl, apparently not many years older than herself. The stranger was dressed in white, and seemed to glide. Her face was white as the snow which capped Mount Daimugenzan; her brows were crescent-shaped, like those of Buddha; her mouth was like flowers. In a silvery voice she called to Okureha, saying:

'Be neither surprised nor afraid, my child. I saw that you were in danger, and I came to your rescue by putting that savage creature to sleep; I sent the warm breeze so that you might not fall. You need not fear that the man is dead. I can revive him if I choose, or keep him as he is if I wish. What is your name?'

Okureha fell on her knees to express her thanks, and, rising, said: 'My name is Okureha. My father is the samurai who owns the greater part of the village of Tashiro, at the foot of the mountain. My mother being ill, I have come up to this old shrine to pray Kwannon for her recovery. Five times have I been up before, but never met any one until today, when this dreadful man attacked me. I owe my deliverance entirely to you, holy lady, and I am humbly and deeply grateful. I do hope I shall be able to come here and pray at this shrine again. My father and mother prayed here before I was born both to Kwannon and to the Tennin of the mountain. They had no child, and I was sent to them after their prayers. Therefore it is right that I should come here to pray for my mother; but this horrid man has frightened me so that I shall be afraid to come alone again.'

The Mountain Goddess (for such was Okureha's rescuer) smiled, and said: 'You need have no fear, my pretty child. Come here when you will, and I shall be your protector. Children who are as devoted to their parents as you are deserve all that is good, and are holy in themselves. If you wish to please me, come again to-morrow, so that we may converse; and bring me some flowers from the fields, for I never descend low enough on earth to get these, though they are my favourites—they smell so sweet. And now you had better go home. When you have had time to reach there I will restore this horrid man to life and let him go. He is not likely to return to molest you.'

'I shall be here to-morrow,' said Okureha, bowing her thanks amid her 'Sayonaras.'

Okureha San was so much impressed by the face of the Goddess that she could not sleep, and at daybreak next morning was out in the fields gathering flowers, which she took up the mountain to the shrine, where she found the goddess waiting.

They talked on many subjects, and enjoyed each other's company, and arranged to meet often. Consequently, whenever Okureha had time she always went up the mountain. This continued for nearly a year, when Okureha went up with flowers for the goddess as usual; but she was looking sad, and felt sad.

'Why is this?' asked the goddess. 'Why are you so sad?'

'Ah, your Holiness is right,' said Okureha. 'I am sad, for this may be the last day I can come up here and see you. I am now seventeen years of age, and my parents think me old enough to marry. Twelve years ago my father arranged that I should marry

97

the son of one of his friends, Tokue, of Iwasakimura, when we were old enough. Now I am said to be old enough: so I must marry. The wedding is to be in three days. After that I shall have to stay at home and work for my husband, and I fear I shall not see you any more. That is why I am sad.' As she spoke tears ran down her cheeks, and there was for a few moments no consoling her; but the goddess soothed her, saying:

'You must not be sad, dear child. On the contrary, you are about to enter the happiest state of life, by being married. If people were not married, and did not produce children to inherit new spirits and life, there could be no continuation. Go back, my child, happily; get married and produce children. You will be happy and doing your duty to the world and to the goddess. Before we say farewell, I give you this small gourd of furoshu. Take care of it on your way down the mountain, and when you are married give some to your husband. You will both remain as you are in appearance, never growing a day older though you live for centuries, as you will do; and also it will bring you perfect happiness. Now, farewell!'

Again the tears came to Okureha's eyes as she bade farewell to her benefactress; but she mustered all her pluck, and, making her last bow, took her way down the mountain, weeping as she went. Three days later Okureha was married. It was a lucky day according to the calendars, and, moreover, it was the year that the Emperor Toba came to the throne, 1108 A.D.

One day, when celebrating this event at a picnic, Okureha gave her husband some of the furoshu saké, and took the rest herself, as the goddess had bidden her. They were sitting on a beautiful green grassy spot, whereon grew wild violets of delicious fragrance; at their feet gurgled a mountain stream of sparkling clearness. To their surprise, they found petals of cherry blossom suddenly falling all round them. There were no cherry trees near, and at first they were much puzzled; but they saw in the blue sky one white cloud which had just sailed over them,

98

and seated thereon was the Goddess of Mount Daimugenzan. Okureha recognised her, and pointed her out to her husband as their benefactress. The white cloud carried her up to the top of the mountain, where it hovered until the shades of evening hid it.

Okureha and her husband never grew older. They lived for hundreds of years as Sennins in Mount Daimugenzan.

***

The style of storytelling most frequently employed in both shamanic stories and in fairy tales is that of magic realism, in which although "the point of departure is 'realistic' (recognizable events in chronological succession, everyday atmosphere, verisimilitude, characters with more or less predictable psychological reactions), ... soon strange discontinuities or gaps appear in the 'normal,' true-to-life texture of the narrative" (Calinescu, 1978, p.386). In other words, what happens is that our expectations based on our intuitive knowledge of physics are ultimately breached and knocked out. It is the style of storytelling that we find in this particular tale as, right from the outset, we are given precise details of the location of the mountain, "Between the north-eastern boundary of Totomi Province and the north-western of Suruga Province", and also the approximate year in which the event took place - about 1107 A.D. These details provide the realistic point of departure referred to above.

The shaman is often characterized by the distinctive ability to shape-shift, and this is what the goddess of the mountain does, first appearing to Okureha in the form of "a beautiful girl, apparently not many years older than herself. The stranger was dressed in white, and seemed to glide. Her face was white as the snow which capped Mount Daimugenzan; her brows were crescent-shaped, like those of Buddha; her mouth was like flowers."

Sometimes the shift that takes place is a literal one, human flesh transformed into animal flesh or covered over by animal skin; in other accounts, the soul leaves the shaman's unconscious body to enter into the body of an animal, fish or bird. However, not all transformations are from human to animal shape. In Tibet, for example, a frog-husband is an unexpected source of joy to a shy young bride. He is not a man disguised as a frog but a frog disguised as a man. When his young wife burns his frog skin to keep her lover in the shape she prefers, the frog-husband loses his magical powers, gracefully resigning himself to ordinary human life instead.

It is not only shamans who have such powers according to tales from around the globe. Shape shifting is part of a mythic and story-telling tradition stretching back over thousands of years. The gods of various mythologies are credited with this ability, as are the heroes of the great epic sagas. In Nordic myth, Odin could change his shape into any beast or bird; in Greek myth, Zeus often assumed animal shape in his relentless pursuit of young women. Cernunnos, the lord of animals in Celtic mythology, wore the shape of a stag, and also the shape of a man with a heavy rack of horns.

"Shamanic journeys frequently involve passing through some kind of gateway, and it is the shrine to Kwannon on the sacred mountain that represents the gateway between the two worlds here, and the starting point for Okureha's journey.". As for the drinking of the wine, which brings about the transformation of Okureha and her husband, it can be seen to represent their initiatory rite into the world of the spirits.

What follows is a guided visualisation based on the story presented above. If you are working on your own, it is suggested that you record the script, perhaps with some appropriate background music. You can then lie somewhere comfortable, where you will not be disturbed, and play the recording back to yourself as you go through the process described.

SCRIPT FOR THE GUIDE: (To be read in a gentle trance-inducing voice). Make yourself comfortable and close your eyes. Take a few deep breaths to help you relax. Feel the tension disappear stage by stage from the top of your head to the tips of your toes. Let your surroundings fade away as you gradually sink backwards through time and actuality and pass through the gateway of this reality into the dreamtime. (When the participants are fully relaxed, begin the next stage).

You find yourself standing at the foot of Mount Daimugenzan, a place of power, where many have come before you for, and where many will no doubt come after you. And you know, whatever your problem is, that it is here you will find help, and that is what has brought you to this place.

It is a wild and rugged mountain, its lower reaches clad with lofty pines. Ahead of you there's a winding path, leading up to the summit. The scent from the pine trees is carried by the breeze and fills the air. The climb is steep but you're determined and refuse to be deterred. And the higher you climb, the stronger your resolve becomes - the resolve you have to achieve what you have set out to do.

About half-way up through the forest, you eventually come to the shrine erected to Kwannon; but it is so small that no priest lives there, the building is rotting away, and you find yourself all alone there. The silence all around envelops you and you feel at peace and in harmony with the world. And so you take a minute of clock time, equal to all the time you need, to appreciate the sense of balance you feel ...

And now advancing towards you, comes a beautiful girl. The stranger is dressed in white, and seems to glide. Her face is white as the snow which caps the mountain you are on; her brows are crescent-shaped, like those of Buddha; her mouth is like flowers. In a silvery voice she calls to you.

'Be neither surprised nor afraid. I saw you were in trouble, that you had lost your way in life, and so I have come to you to offer help.'

In her hands, the goddess holds a silver goblet, and she passes it to you to drink from. And, as you know, whosoever drinks of it will live forever in that their spirit for life will be rekindled and never die again. This is the moment you have been waiting for. And, as you raise the goblet to your lips, take a minute of clock time, equal to all the time you need, to appreciate the renewed spirit it fills you with, like liquid crystal running through your veins ...

And you know now, with an unfailing certainty, such as you have never experienced before, that never again will life seem to be nothing more than a chore to you, that never again will you feel that you can't go on. For, refreshed and revitalised, you know now that you will never grow tired of life again, and that as a result, you are now able to act and move forward once more. So take a minute of clock time, equal to all the time you need, to reflect on what it is you have blessed with today ...

And now that the purpose of your journey has been accomplished, now that your spirit has been rekindled, the time has come to give thanks to the goddess of the mountain and to make your way back home, back, back, down the side of the mountain, through the forest of pine trees, back, back, down to the place where you stood when you first set out on your journey and back to the place you started from.

Take a deep breath, let it all out slowly, open your eyes, and smile at the first person you see. Stretch your arms, stretch your legs, stamp your feet on the ground, and make sure you're really back, back in ..., back where you started from. Welcome home!

Now take a few minutes in silence to make some notes on the experiences you had on your journeys, which you can then share with the rest of the group.

Or

Now take a few minutes in silence to make some notes on the

experiences you had on your journeys, which you can then make a note of in your dream journal.

Or

And now you might like to turn to the person sitting next to you and share some of the experiences you had on your journeys

References

Calinescu, M. (1978) 'The Disguises of Miracle: Notes on Mircea Eliade's Fiction.' In Bryan Rennie (ed.) (2006) *Mircea Eliade: A Critical Reader*, London: Equinox Publishing Ltd.

Eliade, M. (2003) *Rites and Symbols of Initiation*, Putnam, Connecticut: Spring Publications (originally published by Harper Bros., New York, 1958).

Smith, R.G. (1918) *Ancient Tales and Folklore of Japan*, London, A. & C. Black. Scanned at sacred-texts.com, February 2006. Edited and Proofed by John Bruno Hare. This text is in the public domain in the United States because it was published prior to January 1st, 1923. These files may be used for any non-commercial purpose provided this notice of attribution is left intact in all copies.

What is Shamanic Counselling
and How Much is it Worth?

What is shamanism and can it be classified as a religion? What is
core shamanic counselling and what services do its practitioners
offer? Should it be charged for? Can a price be put on spiritual
goods or are they priceless? This chapter will attempt to provide
answers to these questions, in part through the use of storytelling.

First of all, what is shamanism and what is a shaman? There
are as many definitions on offer as there are writers on the
subject, but this is what I would like to propose:

> A shaman can be defined as someone who performs an
> ecstatic (in a trance state), imitative, or demonstrative ritual of
> a séance (or a combination of all three), at will (in other words,
> whenever he or she chooses to do so), in which aid is sought
> from beings in (what are considered to be) other realities
> generally for healing purposes or for divination – both for
> individuals and / or the community[3].

Though it is hoped that the definition is deliberately broad
enough to accommodate the variations that exist between
shamanistic communities, both indigenous and neo-shamanic,
some would argue that different definitions are required for both.
However, it surely has to be accepted it is no longer possible to
make a watertight distinction between the two. 'For shamanism,
as with any other kind of local knowledge, the essence of
globality today is that it belongs both in the past of remote tribes,
and in the present of industrial sub-cultures' (Vitebsky, 1993, p.3).
In other words, there are no longer any clear dividing lines,
which is why only one definition is being proposed.

As for the argument of whether shamanism can be classified as a religion or not, it will be referred to as "a religion of ritual observance", centred on the dramatization of the death and resurrection of the shaman in whom the well-being of the client and sometimes of the whole community rests.

The phrase "a religion of ritual observance" has been used in particular to describe Shinto – 'a religion not of theology but of ritual observance' (Driver, 1991, p.38). However, it would seem to me that much the same could be said of shamanism. The advantage of this description is it could not offend either New-Agers who might consider the term "religion" without any form of qualification to be an unacceptable word to describe what they practise, or members of the predominant religions who might consider, for various reasons, that shamanism should not be included among their number (see Berman, 2006, p.80).

Now for what core shamanic counselling consists of. Among his other achievements, Michael Harner can be credited with having developed a way of using shamanic techniques in the field of counselling. Harner Method Shamanic Counseling is a system that enables clients to make their own journeys to non-ordinary reality to obtain guidance in answer to the questions most important in their lives, and the client is counselled to become his or her own shaman for this type of journey. The use of a drumming tape [played through a set of earphones] ... permits the shamanic counsellor to utilize ... the technique of *simultaneous narration*, wherein the client is asked to narrate out loud [into a microphone] the details of his or her journey as it is happening' (Doore, 1988, p.180). The recording makes it possible to carry out an immediate review and analysis of the experience and of the information gained. Harner regards the system as a method of personal empowerment by means of which we can recognize our own ability to acquire spiritual guidance without having to depend on external mediators. 'The whole idea is to return to people what was once taken away from them when the state began perpetuating monopolies on access to spiritual knowledge' (Doore, 1988, p.181). The Harner Method can be described as a form of brief therapy that aims to help people to help themselves. Unfortunately, however successful the method is in practice, its respectability is called into question by the fact that the training to become a certified Counsellor (available from the Foundation for Shamanic Studies) cannot be compared to the study involved in becoming a qualified psychotherapist, for example. This is a problem it shares with other forms of alternative or non-conventional treatment, regardless of whether they work or not.

Sandra Ingerman, who has worked with Harner, specializes in utilizing the technique of soul retrieval as a form of therapy, which is another service offered by practitioners of the Harner method. Soul in this context can be characterized as being our vital essence, where the emotions, feeling or sentiments are situated. The aim of soul retrieval is to recover the part of the client's soul that has been lost as this causes an "opening" through which illness can enter. The cause of this loss is believed to be due to an emotional or physical trauma that the client has been through. Ingerman believes it is the shaman's role to track down the lost soul part in non-ordinary reality and then to return it to the body (see Ingerman, 1993, p.23).

For a more complete picture of the services a core shamanic counsellor offers, here are descriptions taken from the website **www.shamanicpractitioners.org.uk** written by three practitioners who trained with Jonathan Horwitz – founder of the Scandinavian Centre for Shamanic Studies:

I practice [this spelling mistake is on the website] shamanic healing including soul and power animal retrieval and extraction work. I also do divinatory journeys for people. Connection to oneself, to others and to the world we live in is both sacred and vital for our well-being. One of the beliefs that shamanic societies all over the world share is that everything is alive, sacred and connected. A lot of my work is focused around issues of restoring a sense of that connection.

If we allow the pressures and stresses of "modern life" to build up, or we ignore our inner needs, we can become susceptible to negative energies or illnesses which can affect our daily lives. As a shamanic practitioner, I work with my spirit guides and helpers to diagnose the source of the issues brought to me, and to use soul and power retrieval, extraction and ritual work to bring release from blockages and to promote inner wellbeing. If you feel this might be helpful to you, I am always happy to have an initial discussion by email or telephone without obligation.

"After a widely wandering spiritual journey I found shamanism, and it felt like coming home! I have worked shamanically for over 8 years and offer shamanic healing, soul retrieval, counselling and journeying - or any other way my spirits ask me to work with people! With the CSPC I have recently undertaken research work into shamanism and homoeopathy - understanding and experiencing plant, animal and mineral spirit remedies in a deeper and more connected way. This work continues and I now teach homoeopaths how to work shamanically with remedies, as well as teaching occasional workshops for all. I like to work in a very grounded way, with regular practice in nature, as for me the whole power of shamanism is found in bringing the advice, healing and information given into our ordinary lives in order to live more extraordinarily and with a deeper connection with our Universe."

www.shamanicpractitioners.org.uk [accessed 28/3/08]

Their initial training would have consisted of perhaps three weekend workshops followed by a residential week. However, it should be pointed out that Jonathan carefully vets trainees before accepting them on to the training course, and that both the practitioners whose services are described above do have considerable experience.

There is a fundamental difference, which has been observed by Wallis, between the neo-shamanism advocated by Harner and indigenous shamanism. In the former, the emphasis is very much on control, with its promises that the technique is safe to practitioners, and he concludes that this reveals the Western need to be in control (over consciousness, emotions, or money) even though nothing like this may be found in indigenous shamanism (Wallis, 1999, p.46). On the other hand, it should be pointed out in Harner's defence, he makes no claim that what he teaches is indigenous shamanism. The reason for the emphasis on control in core-shamanism could well be twofold. Not only does it ensure the practices are made safe and suitable for teaching on workshops, but it also shows shamanism in a more positive light following the decades of oppression it has had to contend with in indigenous communities by colonising cultures and religions (see Wallis, 2003, p.54).

It would initially seem from the following quote that Villoldo, another neo-shamanic practitioner who offers training programmes, does at least recognize the dangers that can be involved in what he does and teaches, the eristic nature of shamanic practices: 'There are dangers associated with energy healing, both for the client and for the healer. Far too many poorly trained practitioners dispense energy healing without understanding the mechanics of the human energy field' (Villoldo, 2001, p.2). Villoldo then goes on to pose the following question: 'A doctor of Western medicine spends at least five years learning his or her craft. Is it prudent to turn my health care over to someone who has taken a weekend workshop in energy medicine?' (Villoldo, 2001, p.6).

Yet if you visit Villoldo's website, **www.thefourwinds.com**, you learn that his 'professional training program ... leading to certification in luminous healing and energy medicine ... [in which] You will learn the mystery teachings (the work of the Medicine Wheel), the Illumination Process, The Extraction Process, Soul Retrieval, and the Great Rites, ceremonies that assist in one's life passage' actually consists of only a basic four weeks of training over two years. Consequently, it is highly debatable whether he actually puts into practice what he preaches.

The expensive "crash courses" offered by neo-shamanists have come in for a lot of criticism from purists. However, Harner has countered such criticisms with the following argument: 'If the nation states of the world are working day and night on a crash course of their own for our mutual annihilation, we cannot afford to be any slower in our work in the opposite direction' (Harner, 1990, p.81). This defence was particularly pertinent at the time it was proposed as it came just after the accident at Chernobyl nuclear plant in 1986.

On the other hand, what cannot necessarily be justified is the high cost involved, though it has to be admitted that the courses are at least a lot cheaper than those teaching, for example, the principles of Neuro-Linguistic Programming. To make matters worse, the promotional material advertising NLP courses (as I know from the unsolicited junk mail that keeps arriving in the post) frequently refers to the cost as an "investment" in view of the undoubted benefits that can be derived from such training. However, this can only be a matter of opinion – the opinion of those who profit financially from what is being offered.

The views of Horwitz on charging fees for counselling individual clients are worth including at this point as he makes out a convincing case in favour of the practice. The following is an extract from an e-mail he sent me on the subject:

As to the payment angle, yes it is a difficult nut to crack. In our culture we think spiritual work=free. But I've never heard of a traditional culture where the shaman wasn't paid. People knew to do it. They just brought what they could, three horses, a freshly killed deer, sometimes a child to be a servant-apprentice, even a wife. That kind of thing doesn't go in our culture. I do feel there should be an exchange of energy, as it were. I feel 2 hours of my time is very valuable. Time is the most precious thing I have. I feel if I am going to give 2 hours of my and my Spirits undivided attention, 2 hours of my life, then the one who gets that attention should give something, too. Most people would rather give me money than clean my house for 2 hours. Some would rather clean my house. I don't care. I know X [I have removed the person's name to protect her confidentiality] has paid a lot in many different ways to get where she has gotten to after following a spiritual path for more than 15 years. If her Spirits say it's ok for her to get £45 for a 2 hour session, who am I to argue? The saddest thing about this is that some people don't respect the work unless they have to pay for it! Ah, well, what to do? If you were seeing 5 or 6 people each week (10 to 15 hours) wouldn't you want some sort of compensation. I knew a psychologist when I lived in New York who saw 12 people everyday for 45 minute hours. He took $100 an hour. Where is the line? These are questions we have to answer for ourselves – or ask our Spirits.

As an English Language teacher who charges the private students I teach on an occasional basis fees, it would be wrong for me to criticize the counsellor referred to in the letter above for doing the same. The question of whether she is skilful or qualified enough to be offering such services for money is a different matter though. Not knowing her, I am not in a position to comment on that. However, if this form of therapy were to become accredited by the State with an approved list of practitioners being established, such issues would no longer pose a problem. The likelihood of that happening would appear to be a long way off though.

There is a tradition of charging for spiritual services and it can be argued that even gods have been known to do so. For example, in return for saving Jonah from the "whale", his god subsequently required him to prophesy to the Ninevites – payment in kind. However, can the god of the Children of Israel and a neo-shamanic practitioner really be compared? It is obvious how "outsiders" would answer this question.

I would suggest that instead of attempting to regulate or even prohibit shamanic practitioners, as some would favour, we should leave it to the consciences of the practitioners themselves as to what they offer, and the process of supply and demand. For if they prove unable to provide the services they advertise, there will presumably be no demand for them in any case. Instead of asking what the monetary value of spiritual services is perhaps we should be asking what the value of knowledge is. The traditional Chinese tale that follows and concludes this chapter offers a possible answer:

Loss of Memory

Hua Tzu of the state of Sung suffered from a loss of memory in his middle years. Whatever he took in the morning was forgotten by the evening and whatever he gave in the evening was forgotten by the morning. On the road he would forget to move ahead and indoors he would forget to sit down. As his wife used to say, here and now he has forgotten then, and later he will not remember the here and now.

He consulted an astrologer, but divination provided no answer. Then he sought the help of a medium, but prayer could not control the problem either. Finally he visited a doctor, but once again the treatment brought no relief.

Now in the state of Lu there was a Confucian scholar who claimed that he could cure the disease, and Hua Tzu's wife paid him half their estate to do it. "No sign or omen," said the Confucian, "can solve this. No prayer can preserve him and no medicine will work. I must try to transform his mind, alter his way of thinking, and then there may be hope." The scholar stripped Hua Tzu, and the naked man demanded clothes. The scholar starved Hua Tzu, and he demanded food. He locked Hua Tzu in a dark room, and he demanded light.

"This illness can be cured," the Confucian advised Hua Tzu's son. "But my remedy is a secret handed down for generations, a secret that has never been revealed to anyone outside our family. I must ask you to dismiss all your father's attendants so that he can live alone with me for seven days." The son agreed.

Nobody knows what methods the scholar used, but Hua Tzu's ailment of many years miraculously cleared up. But when Hua Tzu realized that he was cured, he flew into a tremendous rage. He chastised his wife, punished his son, and drove off the Confucian with weapons. People seized Hua Tzu and asked him the reason for his strange behaviour.

"In my forgetfulness I was a free man, unaware if heaven and earth even existed," said Hua Tzu. "But now I remember all that has passed, all that remains, all that was gained or lost, all that brought sorrow or joy, all that was loved or hated – the ten thousand problems that have plagued my life. And I fear that these same things will disturb my mind no less in times to come. Where shall I find another moment's peace? That's the reason why."

References

Berman, M. (2005) *The Shaman & the Storyteller*, Powys: Superscript.

Berman, M. (2006) 'The Nature of Shamanism and the Shamanic Journey', unpublished M.Phil Thesis, University of Wales, Lampeter.

Doore, G. (ed.) (1988) *Shaman's Path: Healing, Personal Growth and Empowerment*, Boston, Massachusetts: Shambhala Publications.

Driver, T.F. (1991) *The Magic of Ritual*, New York: Harper Collins Publishers.

Foundation for Shamanic Studies **http://www.shamanism.org**

Ingermann, S. (1991) *Soul Retrieval: Mending the Fragmented Self through Shamanic Practice*, San Francisco: Harper.

Ingermann, S. (1993) *Welcome Home: Following Your Soul's Journey Home*, New York: Harper Collins Publishers.

Roberts, M. (1979) *Chinese Fairy Tales & Fantasies*, New York: Pantheon Books.

Scandinavian Centre for Shamanic Studies **http://www.shaman-center.dk**

Villoldo, A. (2001) *Shaman Healer Sage*, London: Bantam Books.

Vitebsky, P. (1993) 'Shamanism as Local Knowledge in a Global Setting: from Cosmology to Psychology and Environmentalism' – a Paper presented at the ASA IV Decennial Conference.

Vitebsky, P. (2001) *The Shaman*, London: Duncan Baird (first published in Great Britain in 1995 by Macmillan Reference Books).

Wafer, J. (1991) *The Taste of Blood: Spirit Possession in Brazilian Candomblé*. University of Pennsylvania Press.

Wallis, R.J. (2003) *Shamans/Neo-shamans*, London: Routledge.

Thomas the Rhymer and
the Queen of Elfland

Glosecki maintains that there could well be a shamanic past behind *Beowulf* and other Old English poems and that early poetry could well be an art form rooted in tribal tradition that therefore retains traces of native beliefs.

> [T]he living body of shamanic belief could not survive accelerated cultural changes especially Christianization. But on the other hand, this elaborate magico-religious system – instilled in the *mythos*, ingrained in the language inherent in the medicine – could not die out quickly, either, among those mobile tribes whose settlements eventually grew into the Germanic nations of feudal Europe. In particular, images of the old animal guardians died out very slowly; they recur in the art as reflexes of the native symbol system that could be superseded, but not eradicated (Glosecki, 1989, p.1).

Whether these beliefs persisted after the introduction of Christianity, but to a greatly reduced extent, or died out and were then re-invented with the neo-shamanic movement, we have no way of knowing for sure. What we can be sure of, however, is that "too many reflexes occur in the literature for us to ignore the influential role shamanism played in Anglo-Saxon prehistory" (ibid.p.3), and how it went on to influence later poetry / ballads too.

Thomas Rhymer, Child Ballad 37, is traceable back at least as far as the 13th century and there are several different variants of the story. Most, however, have the same basic theme - that Thomas either kissed or had sex with the Queen of Fairyland and either rode with her or was otherwise transported to Fairyland. One version relates that she changed into a hag immediately after sleeping with him, as some sort of a punishment to him, but returned to her originally beautiful state when they neared her castle, where her husband lived. Thomas stayed at a party in the castle, until she told him to return with her, coming into the mortal realm only to realise seven years had passed (a significant number in magic). He asked for a token to remember the Queen by, and was then offered the choice of being a harper or a prophet, and chose the latter. He became known as true Thomas, because he could not tell a lie, and was popularly supposed to have prophesised many great events in Scottish history. His gift of prophecy seems to have been related to that of poetry, as Thomas was a noted poet (hence, "Rhymer"), and was supposed to have written the ballad of *St Tristrem*. After a number of years had passed Thomas returned to fairyland, where he is still said to be.

Records show that the character of Thomas in the ballad was in fact based on a historical figure. Thomas Learmonth (c. 1220 – c.1298; also spelled Learmount, Learmont, or Learmounth), better known as Thomas the Rhymer or True Thomas, was a 13th century Scottish laird and reputed prophet from Earlston (then called "Erceldoune"). On the southern edge of the village there are the remains of an old keep dating back to the 1400s, called "Rhymer's Tower" because they are believed to stand on the site of the castle originally built by Thomas the Rhymer.

Thomas the Rhymer's reputation for making prophesies is said to include a prediction of the death of Alexander III in a fall from a horse in 1286. This prediction was apparently made to the Earl of March in Dunbar Castle the day before the accident happened. According to some sources Thomas is also said to have had other supernatural powers that even rivalled those of Merlin. It is said that on visiting Fyvie Castle in Aberdeenshire, a freak gust of wind shut the gates in his face, and in response he placed the "curse of the weeping stones" on the castle, a curse which has led to problems of succession down through the centuries as an unusually large number of different families have occupied the castle.

As for the spot where Thomas is believed to have fallen asleep under the Eildon Tree, it is now marked by what is known as the Rhymer's Stone and can be seen today by all who visit the village.

Thomas Rymer

TRUE THOMAS lay oer yond grassy bank,
And he beheld a ladie gay,
A ladie that was brisk and bold,
Come riding oer the fernie brae.

Her skirt was of the grass-green silk,
Her mantel of the velvet fine,
At ilka tett of her horse's mane
Hung fifty silver bells and nine.

True Thomas he took off his hat,
And bowed him low down till his knee:
'All hail, thou mighty Queen of Heaven!
For your peer on earth I never did see.'

'O no, O no, True Thomas,' she says,
'That name does not belong to me;
I am but the queen of fair Elfland,
And I'm come here for to visit thee.

'But ye maun go wi me now, Thomas,
True Thomas, ye maun go wi me,
For ye maun serve me seven years,
Thro weel or wae as may chance to be.'

She turned about her milk-white steed,
And took True Thomas up behind,
And aye wheneer her bridle rang,
The steed flew swifter than the wind.

For forty days and forty nights
He wade thro red blude to the knee,
And he saw neither sun nor moon,
But heard the roaring of the sea.

O they rade on, and further on,
Until they came to a garden green:
'Light down, light down, ye ladie free,
Some of that fruit let me pull to thee.'

'O no, O no, True Thomas,' she says,
'That fruit maun not be touched by thee,
For a' the plagues that are in hell
Light on the fruit of this countrie.

'But I have a loaf here in my lap,
Likewise a bottle of claret wine,
And now ere we go farther on,
We'll rest a while, and ye may dine.'

When he had eaten and drunk his fill,
'Lay down your head upon my knee,'
The lady sayd, re we climb yon hill,
And I will show you fairlies three.

'O see not ye yon narrow road,
So thick beset wi thorns and briers?
That is the path of righteousness,
Tho after it but few enquires.

'And see not ye that braid braid road,
That lies across yon lillie leven?
That is the path of wickedness,
Tho some call it the road to heaven.

'And see not ye that bonny road,
Which winds about the fernie brae?
That is the road to fair Elfland,
Whe[re] you and I this night maun gae.

'But Thomas, ye maun hold your tongue,
Whatever you may hear or see,
For gin ae word you should chance to speak,
You will neer get back to your ain countrie.'

He has gotten a coat of the even cloth,
And a pair of shoes of velvet green,
And till seven years were past and gone
True Thomas on earth was never seen.

***

We first meet Thomas lying on a grassy bank, presumably resting, daydreaming, or maybe even sleeping – in other words, a trance like state. To make a shamanic journey requires a change in one's mode of being, entering a transcendent state, which makes it possible to attain the world of spirit, and that is what Thomas can be seen to do. The fact that the lady's horse has fifty nine bells hanging from it marks here out as being different in some way, traditionally one of the marks of a shaman, as does the respectful way in which Thomas acknowledges her. We should also point out that one of the traditional attributes of the shaman is also his or her ability to communicate with the animals, and the horse is frequently the form of transport used by the shaman to access other worlds.

> Pre-eminently the funerary animal and psychopomp, the "horse" is employed by the shaman, in various contexts, as a means of achieving ecstasy, that is, the "coming out of oneself" that makes the mystical journey possible. This mystical journey–to repeat–is not necessarily in the infernal direction. The "horse" enables the shaman to fly through the air, to reach the heavens. The dominant aspect of the mythology of the horse is not infernal but funerary; the horse is a mythical image of death and hence is incorporated into the ideologies and techniques of ecstasy. The horse carries the deceased into the beyond; it produces the "break-through in plane," the passage from this world to other worlds (Eliade, 1964, p.467).

As has already been pointed out in this volume, the style of storytelling most frequently employed in both shamanic stories and in fairy tales is that of magic realism, in which although "the point of departure is 'realistic' (recognizable events in chronological succession, everyday atmosphere, verisimilitude, characters with more or less predictable psychological reactions), … soon strange discontinuities or gaps appear in the 'normal,' true-to-life texture of the narrative" (Calinescu, 1978, p.386). In other words, what happens is that our expectations based on our intuitive knowledge of physics are ultimately breached and knocked out. It is also the style of storytelling we can find employed in ballads. In *Thomas Rhymer*, for example, verisimilitude is established by providing us with the name of the location of where Thomas was found, and by furnishing us with details of the precise number of bells to be found on the horse's mane.

In the context of the spiritual interpretation of entry into fairyland, whichever method the fairy employed to bring the human into their world, and for whatever reason they wanted them there, the fairy would have been, in effect, desiring and appropriating (for a given length of time) the human spirit or soul. In the same context, those individuals who were tempted to enter fairyland voluntarily, for whatever reason, would have been aware that their visit amounted to a temporary, albeit tacit, commitment of their soul to (be used / enjoyed by) the fairies – a transaction which amounted to an implicit contract (Wilby, 2005, p.104).

In the case of Thomas Rhymer, he was tempted into fairyland by his love for a fairy woman. As to the nature of fairyland, "Fairy society, like that of early modern Britain, was presided over by a monarchy, and the fairy king and queen, sometimes accompanied by an entourage of aristocratic henchmen, reigned over a mannered and lavish court" (Wilby, 2005, p.19).

The shamanic journey frequently involves passing through some kind of gateway. As Eliade explains,

The "clashing of rocks," the "dancing reeds," the gates in the shape of jaws, the "two razor-edged restless mountains," the "two clashing icebergs," the "active door," the "revolving barrier," the door made of the two halves of the eagle's beak, and many more – all these are images used in myths and sagas to suggest the insurmountable difficulties of passage to the Other World [and sometimes the passage back too] (Eliade, 2003, pp.64-65).

The forty days and nights are of course a reference to the biblical story of Noah, and help to convey the epic and momentous nature of the journey Thomas undertakes, and the gateway between the worlds that Eliade refers to is the red blood Thomas is required to wade through on the way. The river of blood may also be a biblical reference - to the blood and water that flowed from the wound in Christ's side.

The fact that Thomas is forbidden to eat any of the fruit on the trees is not only another biblical reference, in this case to the story of Adam and Eve, but also to be expected in an account of what is in effect a shamanic journey. When journeying in other realities, partaking of food is often forbidden, especially when journeying through the Land of the Dead (see, for example, Paul Radin's account of the Winnebago Indian Road to the nether world in the Thirty Eighth Annual Report, Bureau of American Ethnology, Washington, DC., 1923, pp. 143-4, which is reproduced in Berman 2007).

For food and drink that can be consumed on the journey without any risk, the Queen of Elfland offers Thomas bread and wine, the body and blood of Christ, and the drink induces a trance like state in him once again, during which he is shown a vision.

Let us now consider why there should be three roads to choose from. Three is linked with the phases of the moon (waxing, full and waning), and with time (past, present and future). Pythagoras called three the perfect number in that it represented the beginning, the middle and the end, and he thus regarded it as a symbol of Deity. The importance of the number in the ballad could well be the result of the influence of Christianity and its use of the Trinity, but it also refers to the three stages in the cycle of life and adds to the universality of the story's appeal.

As to why Thomas should be forbidden to talk of what he will see or hear in Elfland, the reason could be due to the fact that such talk would only be misunderstood by outsiders in any case. Writing or talking about shamanism has always been problematic as "the subject area resists 'objective' analysis and is sufficiently beyond mainstream research to foil ...writing [or talking] about it in a conventional academic way" (Wallis, 2003, p.13). Shamans have their own ways of describing trance experience. Outsidersmight call them 'metaphors', but to shamans these metaphors, such as 'death', are real, lived experiences ... 'Metaphor is a problematic term extracted from Western literary discourse which does not do justice to non-Western, non-literary shamanic experiences. In recognising this limitation, 'metaphor may remain a useful term for explaining alien shamanic experiences in terms understandable to Westerners (Wallis, 2003, p.116).

Perhaps this is why the accounts of memorable shamanic journeys were often turned into folktales or ballads, as it was the only way to make them both understandable and acceptable to people not familiar with the landscapes to be found and experiences to be had in such worlds.

Like the number three, the number seven has symbolic significance too, and the choice of seven years for the time to be spent in Elfland is surely no more arbitrary than the decision to have three roads from:

> Seven is a mystic or sacred number in many different traditions. Among the Babylonians and Egyptians, there were believed to be seven planets, and the alchemists recognized seven planets too. In the Old Testament there are seven days in creation, and for the Hebrews every seventh year was Sabbatical too. There are seven virtues, seven sins, seven ages in the life of man, seven wonders of the world, and the number seven repeatedly occurs in the *Apocalypse* as well. The Muslims talk of there being seven heavens, with the seventh being formed of divine light that is beyond the power of words to describe, and the Kabbalists also believe there are seven heavens—each arising above the other, with the seventh being the abode of God (Berman, 2008, p.122).

Seven may also represent the sun, the moon and the five planets (those known before the invention of the telescope), as astrology has always played an important part in magic too. A common way for witches to acquire magical powers was from encounters with fairies. For example, Anne Jeffries, a 17th century Cornish healer, was found lying unconscious and, when she revived, said that a group of fairies had appeared to her. They continued to visit her regularly, and she found she had acquired healing powers. In this ballad, however, it is Thomas who acquires magical powers this way. He returns to this reality with the power of divination, a traditional attribute of the shaman, and the journey itself can be seen as his shamanic initiation rather than one into witchcraft, which is another possible interpretation of the tale.

"Sceptics will argue that it is impossible to eliminate from analysis the Christian influence on what sources there are available to us, such that we can never be certain in any one case that we are indeed dealing with beliefs that are authentically pagan. This view is now so widely held that we can in justice think of it as the prevailing orthodoxy" (Winterbourne, 2007, p.24). And the same argument could be applied to the attempt to ascertain whether we are dealing with beliefs that are authentically shamanic in *Thomas Rhymer*. Nevertheless, just because a task is difficult is no reason for not attempting it. If it was, then no progress would ever be made in any research that we might be involved in.

To enjoy the journey, it's important to see experiences along the way, both the positive and negative, as steps in the learning process. And as long as you learn from the experiences you have, there is no reason to regard anything untoward that happens along the way as a mistake. It's important to see both successes and failures as events in the unfolding of who we are. (Berman, 2000, p.57)

In the light of the hardships Thomas had to endure on the road to enlightenment, you might now like to reflect on what you have learnt from the adversity you have had to face in your life or lives. As soon as you are able to leave one life behind, the next one has a chance to start. In this way, it is possible to live many in the same lifetime and there is no need to confine yourself to just one. Thomas Rhymer clearly did not and you have no need to do so either.

"The goal of the psychic journey varies widely, although it typically involves *therapy* in a very expansive sense of the term – the "healing" of physical, psychological, or sociological problems" (Glosecki, 1989, p.11). And that is what this book is basically all about - healing brought about through shamanic journeying, through shamanic stories, through shamanic poetry, and through shamanic counselling.

We each have our own magical place or fairyland and, though they may share a lot in common, no two such worlds can be exactly the same. What follows is a poem that describes the fairyland of the Bengali Nobel Prize Winner Rabindranath Tagore, taken from Tagore, R. (1913) *The Crescent Moon*, London and New York: Macmillan and Company.

Fairyland

If people came to know where my king's palace is, it would vanish into the air.

The walls are of white silver and the roof of shining gold.

The queen lives in a palace with seven courtyards, and she wears a jewel that cost all the wealth of seven kingdoms.

But let me tell you, mother, in a whisper, where my king's palace is.

It is at the corner of our terrace where the pot of the *tulsi* plant* stands.

The princess lies sleeping on the far-away shore of the seven impassable seas.

There is none in the world who can find her but myself.

She has bracelets on her arms and pearl drops in her ears; her hair sweeps down upon the floor.

She will wake when I touch her with my magic wand, and jewels will fall from her lips when she smiles.

But let me whisper in your ear, mother; she is there in the corner of our terrace where the pot of the *tulsi* plant stands.

When it is time for you to go to the river for your bath, step up to that terrace on the roof.

I sit in the corner where the shadows of the walls meet together.

Only puss is allowed to come with me, for she knows where the barber in the story lives.

But let me whisper, mother, in your ear where the barber in the story lives.

It is at the corner of the terrace where the pot of the *tulsi* plant stands.

***

*The '*tulsi*' plant** or Indian holy basil is an important symbol in the Hindu religious tradition. Tulsi is a venerated herb and has many medicinal properties.

References

Berman, M. (2000) *The Power of Metaphor*, Carmarthen: Crown House.

Berman, M. (2007) *The Nature of Shamanism and the Shamanic Story*, Newcastle: Cambridge Scholars Publishing.

Berman, M. (2008) *Divination and the Shamanic Story*, Newcastle: Cambridge Scholars Publishing.

Calinescu, M. (1978) 'The Disguises of Miracle: Notes on Mircea Eliade's Fiction.' In Bryan Rennie (ed.) (2006) *Mircea Eliade: A Critical Reader*, London: Equinox Publishing Ltd.

Child, F.J. (1886-98) *The English and Scottish Popular Ballads,* Boston, New York, Houghton, Mifflin and Company. Ballads originally transcribed by Cathy Lynn Preston. HTML Formatting at sacred-texts.com. This text is in the public domain. These files may be used for any non-commercial purpose, provided this notice of attribution is left intact.

Eliade, M. (1964) *Myth and Reality,* London: George Allen & Unwin

Eliade, M. (2003) *Rites and Symbols of Initiation,* Putnam, Connecticut: Spring Publications (originally published by Harper Bros., New York, 1958).

Glosecki, S.O. (1989) *Shamanism and Old English Poetry,* New York: Garland Publishing Inc.

Radin, P. (1923) *The Winnebago Tribe,* in Thirty-eighth Annual Report, Bureau of American Ethnology, Washington, D.C.

Wallis, Robert J. (2003) *Shamans/Neo-Shamans: Ecstasy, Alternative Archaeologies and Contemporary Pagans,* London: Routledge.

Wilby, E. (2005) *Cunning Folk and Familiar Spirits: Shamanistic Visionary Traditions in Early Modern British Witchcraft and Magic,* Brighton: Sussex Academic Press.

Winterbourne, A. (2007) *When The Norns Have Spoken: Time and Fate in Germanic Paganism,* Wales: Superscript.

Tvalchit'a: A Shamanic Story from the Republic of Georgia

The number of people who, when they hear the name 'Georgia,' think immediately of a state in the USA whose capital is Atlanta is decreasing fast. And those who know that Georgia (capital Tbilisi) is a small but vibrant country in the Caucasus, with a fantastic climate, and an unequalled reputation for hospitality, polyphonic singing and wine-growing, are fast becoming the majority. Hopefully stories like this one, first translated from Georgian into English by Ketevan Kalandadze, will help to develop this trend even further. Georgian belongs to the Kartvelian group of Iberian-Caucasian languages. The Assyrian manuscript "A book of peoples and countries", written in the fifth century, contains a note that of 73 peoples then known only 14 had a written language. Among these Georgians are mentioned (Latin, Slavic-Cyrillic, Arabian, Indian, Chinese, Japanese, Korean, Ethiopian, Greek, Georgian, Armenian, Jewish, Mongolian and Syrian). The Georgians have their alphabet, the number of letters being the same as the number of sounds, thus spelling and pronunciation are identical. Handwriting and printing are similar. This makes Georgian orthography one of the simplest and most perfect in the world. The Georgian written language was created under the king Parnavaz (III century AD).

***

There lived a rich merchant who did not have any children. One day he said to his wife:

> "I'm going to go to foreign country, and will stay there for ten years. If I don't return after that, it means I'm dead and that you will need to mourn for me."

The same year the merchant left, his wife had a son.

The merchant stayed abroad for fifteen years in fact, by when his son was also fifteen years old. After the agreed time had passed, the wife was expecting him home every day, but as he had not come back she assumed that he was dead, wore black clothes and mourned for him as she was supposed to.

It was at the beginning of the sixteenth year that the merchant eventually decided to go back to his home country. He packed everything he could take with him, made the sign of the cross, said his prayers, and left. First of all, he travelled overland by horse and carriage and then, when he reached the sea, he continued his journey by ship. However, he was not even half way across the water when the ship was stopped by a kaji (a demon, an evil creature), who would not let it pass.

"Dear God, what have I done wrong to deserve this – to be stuck in the middle of the sea and unable to get back home after having been away from my family for fifteen years?" the merchant complained to God.

"Give me what you don't know and I'll let you go straight away" said the devkaji.

"I have a wife - I know, and I have houses - I know. What else can there be that I don't know?" The sad merchant wondered. Finally he shouted:

"Take it and let me go to see my family in safety."

"OK. I'll let you go then, but only on condition you remember that what you don't know has to come to me by itself. And don't dare think about breaking your word for, if you do, I will flood your whole country!" The kaji threatened him.

So the ship set sail again, and when the merchant eventually stepped ashore, he sent a messenger to his wife, saying that he was returning.

The wife and her son immediately took a carriage and went to meet him half way. The wife hugged her long-missed husband.

"This is your son, he is already fifteen, and he was born the same year you left," said the wife.

It was then that the merchant remembered the promise he had made to the Kaji and grew very sad – "I had a son and I gave him to someone else."

When they got home, the merchant would not eat or drink and would not talk either.

"What's wrong? Why are so sad? Did you get upset because you have a son?" His wife asked.

"Don't ask me," the husband replied.

"I want to find out if you are happy or sad that you have a son."

"Because I didn't know about him I gave him to someone else, and that's why I'm sad," said the merchant, and he then went on to tell her the whole story about what had happened on the ship.

"Have you been given a time limit father?" The son asked.

"Only a year, and after that I need to send you to him."

"Not to worry for this year then father. And then I'll go, and you'll think that you never even had a son."

The year flies past and, before they know it, the time has come for the merchant to hand his son over to the kaji.

"Father, now tell where and to whom I need to go," said the son.

The father clearly did not want to give his son away but he was very scared of the kaji, and that the threat he had made would come true if he were to disobey him.

"This is the way you need to go, and after a few days you'll reach the sea. There you need to sit down on the beach and these are the words you need to call out there: Kaji of the sea, my father made you a promise and here I am! He will hear your voice, rise out of the sea, and take you."

The boy got ready to leave. He packed a few loaves of bread, a small portion of cheese, kissed his parents goodbye, and then set off. He is walking but does not know where he is going. Eventually he comes to the sea. He is very thirsty, looks around, and finds a stream. He went to the stream, quenched his thirst, ate some bread and cheese, and then lay down for a moment. He was so tired that he fell asleep in seconds. An angel appeared in his dream and this is what he said:

"Why are you lying here? Get up! There's a cave very near here. Go and hide in it. At midday, when it gets very hot, three women, the daughters of the king you are going to, will come there flying. They will take their clothes off, lay them in separate piles, and go swimming in the sea; you need to watch carefully, take the clothes of the youngest sister and hide. And unless she promises to be your wife, don't them give back to her. When the women come out of the sea they will scream so loud that a tree will hit another tree, a stone will hit a stone, and a mountain will hit another mountain. You will be safe, though, as long as you stay in the cave and don't leave it."

At that point the boy woke up. He got up and went to find the cave. After a while he found a black dug-out tunnel. He hid himself there. At midday, when it got very hot, three women came there flying, took their clothes off, lay them in separate piles, and ran into the sea to swim. The boy chose the appropriate moment, emerged from the cave, grabbed hold of the youngest sister's clothes, and went back into the cave again.

Then the older sisters got tired of swimming. They came out of the sea and shouted so loud that trees hit each other, stones hit one another, and two mountains hit each other too. Then they got dressed and flew away.

Meanwhile, the youngest sister carried on splashing around in the sea until, in the end she got tired too. So she came out of the water and started to look for her clothes, but could not find them anywhere. Eventually she realised that someone must have hidden them. She shouted:

"If you are my age, be my brother! If you are my father's age, be my father! But, either way, give me back my clothes please!"

The boy did not say a word and did not show himself to her either. The woman got very upset and shouted out aloud once again:

"Be my husband and I'll be your wife, but give me back my clothes!"

Then the boy emerged from the cave and gave her the clothes. The woman got dressed very quickly and said to him:

"I keep my promises. From today you're my husband and I'm now your wife." The woman took him with her.

They walked a long way or they walked a short way until they came to a marble palace. The woman took the boy to one of the rooms, gave him a good supper, and afterwards asked him:

"Who are you, and where do you come from?"

The boy told her everything. Then the woman said:

"You're going to my father, the king of the sea. Those women you saw are my sisters. We live separately, because our cruel stepmother kicked us out. When you get to my father, he'll ask you to do four things for him. But not to worry about that because I'll help you."

The next day the woman showed the boy her father's house, and the merchant's son went to the Devkaj and said to him:

"Here I am your slave. What do you want me to do then?"

The king of the sea said nothing during the day. At dusk, though, he called him and said:

"Can you see this field? By the morning, from here up to there you have to build a fence - three shoulders in height and one shoulder in width. And if you won't do it, I'll fry you on the fire and eat you!"

The boy said nothing and seemed lost in thought.

"Why are you so sad?" His wife asked.

"Your father ordered me to build a fence, three shoulders in height and one shoulder in width by tomorrow morning. But I'm not a magician, so how am I supposed to do that? And it's not going to build itself in that time, is it?"

"Don't worry about that one – it's easy. There will be more difficult problems to solve," said the woman, trying to calm him down. She brought him some bread, cheese, and wine, gave him a good supper, and after that he fell asleep. Then she took out a red apple from her pocket and said: "My red Arabs, I'm in trouble, and I need you to come to me!"

The nine Arabs appeared the same moment she called them. And this is what the woman said to them:

"In such and such a field you need to build a fence - three shoulders in height and one shoulder in width."

The Arabs disappeared straight away.

The new day dawned. The woman woke the boy up, gave him a pair of overalls and a plasterer's trowel, and said:

"The fence is ready. Go now and start working with the trowel, and make it look as if you're just putting the finishing touches to it."

The boy went and he did what his wife told him to do.

In the morning the king of the sea looked out from his window and, when he saw the fence, he said to his nasty wife:

"Woman, take a look and see what kind of fence my slave has built for us!"

"Dagidges Tvali, your eyes are paying tricks with you! It has not been built by your slave. Your youngest daughter built it," she said, disparagingly.

The king of the sea got angry with her, beat her and said: "You chucked my children out of the house and yet still you blame them! What kind of woman are you?"

The merchant's son was staying with them. At dusk the king called him and said: "Inside the fence you built you now have to grow a special garden: one row of this garden should be blossoming, in another row fruit should be ripening, and in the third row the fruit should be ready to pick."

The boy seemed lost in his thoughts once again.

"Why are you so sad?" His wife asked.

"Your father has now ordered me to grow a special garden inside the fence, one row of this garden should be blossoming, in another row fruit should be ripening, and in the third row the fruit should be ready to pick."

"Don't worry about that – it's easy. There will be more difficult ones to solve,"said the woman, trying to calm him down. "Go and ask him to give you the seeds you need," she said. He did what his wife told him to do. She gave him a good supper and after that he fell asleep. Then she took out a red apple from her pocket and said: "My red Arabs, I'm in trouble, and I need you to come to me once again!"

The nine Arabs appeared the same moment she called them. They woman gave them the seed and this is what she said to them:

"Go, and inside the fence, grow a special garden: one row of that garden should be blossoming, in another row the fruit should be ripening, and in the third row the fruit should be ready to pick."

The Arabs disappeared straight away.

A new day dawned, and inside the fence the special garden was growing. The woman woke the boy up, gave him a pair of overalls, and said:

"Go to that garden and pretend you're picking the ripe fruit."

The boy went. He walks in the garden and here and there picks the ripe fruit. The king looked out from the window and when he saw the garden he was very happy. He said to his wife:

"Woman, take a look and see what kind of garden my slave has grown for us!"

"Dagidges Tvali, your eyes are paying tricks with you! It has not been grown by your slave. Your youngest daughter did it," she said, once again making fun of her husband.

The king of the sea got even angrier with her, and this time he both beat her with a stick and shouted at her:

"Leave my poor daughter alone! Leave her alone you dreadful woman!"

The merchant's son still stayed with them. At dusk the king called him and said:

"You see that sea, don't you? By the morning you have to

build a bridge from elephants' bones. And the bridge needs to be wide enough for the armies of nine different kings to be able to march across it freely."

The boy seemed lost in his thoughts once again.

"Why are you so sad?" His wife asked.

"I was told I need to build a bridge from elephants' bones, wide enough for nine armies of nine different kings to walk across."

"Don't worry about that – it's easy. There will be more difficult ones to solve,"said the woman, trying to calm him down once more.

She brought him some bread, cheese, and wine, and sat down with him at the table; he got drunk and fell asleep. Then she took a red apple from her bosom and said:

"My red Arabs, I'm in trouble, and I need you to come to me!"

The nine Arabs appeared the same moment she called them.

"Go and build a bridge across the sea, wide enough for nine armies of nine different kings to walk across!"

The Arabs disappeared straight away. Very early in the morning she woke the boy up, gave him a pair of overalls to wear and a hammer to hit the bridge with here and there.

In the morning the king looked out from the window, saw the bridge and called his wife:

"See what a bridge our slave has built across the sea!"

"Your eyes are paying tricks on you! It hasn't been built by your slave. Your youngest daughter did it, you misguided old fool!"

This time the king got so angry that he beat her with his shoes.

As for the boy, he stayed with them till the evening.

Now the King had two rashies (magic horses): Tvlatula, as fast as the wind and Tvalchit'a who could prophesize the future. He had Tvaltula with him all the time but Tvalchit'a was in the herd with the rest of the horses. In the evening the king called his slave and said:

"Go to the herd, catch Tvalchit'a, and then bring the horse to me."

The boy left him feeling happy. On his way home he is thinking that he will have no problem catching Tvalchit'a, whatever kind of horse he may be.

When the wife saw her husband looking happy she asked:

"You came home very happy today. What did my father ask you to do this time then?"

"He gave me very easy task this time - to catch Tvlachit'a."

"That, in fact, is the most difficult task of all, but we should still try. Go back to my father and ask him for nine bridles, for nine diamond bridles, a diamond chain and a saddle."

The boy returned and brought back what he was asked for.

The woman gave him a good supper, good wine, made him drunk and put him to sleep. At sunrise she took out another red apple and said:

"My red Arabs, I'm in trouble, and I need you to come to me once again!"

The nine Arabs appeared the same moment she called them. She woke up her husband; they both mounted the Arabs and went to catch the rashi.

The sun was just coming out when they reached the herd in the field. Tvalchit'a was standing separately and looking around suspiciously.

The woman gave the Arabs the ropes and told them:

"Go and catch that horse!"

Tvlachit'a killed with its front hooves each Arab who approached it. In fact, it killed all nine of them. Now it was the turn of the merchant's son. The woman gave him a rope, held a sharp knife in one hand, and said to him:

"I won't be able to stand it if you get killed too. So when I see Tvalchit'a coming towards you, I'll stick the knife into my heart."

They hugged each other and said good-bye. The boy took the rope, prayed for help, and went to catch the horse.

Tvalchit'a called to him from afar:

"I feel sorry for you both. So come and catch me and sit on my back!"

The boy and the woman went to Tvlachit'a, hugged it to show their gratitude, and then mounted the horse. After that, they rode together towards the country on the other side of the sea.

The king of the sea was waiting for his slave anxiously, and when he did not return he said to his wife:

"As he hasn't come back, it means he must have been killed by Tvalchit'a."

"You're wrong again! Your youngest daughter and your slave are sitting on Tvalchit'a and riding at this very moment to another country far away from here."

This time the king believed her, mounted his Tvlatula and rode after them. Half way there Tvlachita asked the boy:

"Look back. Can you see anything?"

The boy looked back and said:

"I can see something, the size of a fly."

"That must be my owner. I will turn myself into a vineyard, will turn the woman into grapes and you into a vine-grower. The king won't be able to recognise us and this way we will be safe."

No sooner had he finished saying these words than they came true. The boy is walking around the grape vine and caring for it.

The king of the sea came to the boy and asked him:

"Have you seen a boy and a woman with a horse recently?"

"I've been working here for a year and seen nobody," said the boy.

The disappointed king went back home again.

The vineyard turned back into Tvalchit'a, the grapes turned back into the woman, and vine-grower into the boy. They mounted Tvalchit'a once again and went on their way.

When the king of the sea got home back, his wife asked him:

"Did you manage to catch up with them then?"

"No!"

"Did you meet anyone on the way?"

"Yes, I did, but only a vine grower; he was looking after his grape vine."

"You foolish man! That vineyard was your horse, the grapes – your daughter and the vine grower – your slave. Why didn't you kill him while you had the chance and cut down the entire grape vine while you were at it too?"

So the king mounted his Tvaltula again and rode after them. Tvlachit'a is running fast but knows that Tvaltula is much faster and that it is impossible to get away.

"Look back. Can you see anything?" Tvalchit'a asked the boy.

"I can see something, the size of a fly."

"That must be my owner. I will turn myself into a church, I'll turn the woman into an icon, and you into a priest."

No sooner had he finished saying these words than they came true. The boy is standing in a church dressed as a priest and praying. The king of the sea came and asked him:

"Have you seen a boy and a woman with a horse recently?"

"I've been here more then a year and I haven't even seen a bird flying here, and certainly not any humans."

The king of the sea left. The church turned back into the horse, the icon into the woman, and the priest into the boy. They mounted Tvalchit'a once again and went on their way.

When the king of the sea got home back, his wife asked him:

"Did you manage to catch up with them then?"

"No!"

"In that case, did you meet anyone on the way?"

"Yes, I did, but only a priest; he was praying in front of an icon."

"You foolish man! That church was your horse, the icon – your daughter and the priest – your slave. Why didn't you destroy the church, break the icon and kill the priest while you had the chance?"

This time the woman made her husband stay at home, and it was she who mounted Tvaltula and set off in pursuit of the boy and the king's youngest daughter.

Thvalchit'a is running fast but Tvlaltual is faster, so there is no way the horse can get away from the king's wife.

"Look back. Can you see anything?" Tvalchit'a asked.

"Someone is galloping like the wind," the merchant's son answered.

Tvalchit'a turned herself into a lake, and the boy and the girl into ducks, paddling on it.

As soon as the cruel wife reached the lake, she dismounted from the horse and started to drink the lake. Little by little she was drinking up the whole lake, and the ducks were following the water towards her mouth. It was nearly the end for them, but the woman's stomach became so full that it burst and she died. Then the lake turned back into Tvalchit'a, and the ducks into the boy and the girl.

"You have to finish off that damn woman once and for all, to chop her up into small pieces; otherwise she will cause even more trouble for us."

So the boy drew out his sword and cut up the kaji woman into tiny pieces. Then one on them sat on Tvlachit'a and the other one on Tvlatula, and they carried on.

Time passed and the woman gave a birth to a girl. The parents decided to give her such a name that nobody would ever be able to guess it, a name that only her parents would know. After careful consideration, they decided to call her 'Dajekala' ("Sitting Down Woman").

The girl grew up and the time came for her to take a husband. The parents decided only to let her marry a man who was able to guess her special name. Many rich men came and tried, but nobody succeeded. One day an Arab, who happened to be passing by, noticed that a large crowd of people had gathered together, and he stopped to ask an old woman why:

"Mother, could you tell me what's happening and why all these people are gathered together here?"

"My son, there is an unmarried girl and her parents will only marry her to a man who can guess her name. That's why all these youngsters are gathered here."

"If I can guess her name, do you think they will give her to me?"

"Yes, they will. Why should you be an exception? They will keep their promise – of that you can be certain."

So the Arab went into the courtyard of the house and shouted:

"I know the name - that woman is called Dajekala!"

The girl's parents kept their promise and gave her to the Arab to be his wife. Dajekala, meanwhile, was crying bitterly and cursing her luck:

"How unlucky I am to have to marry an Arab! What have I done to deserve such luck?"

As distressed as she was at the prospect, there was nothing at all she could do about it. She could not possibly go against her parents' wishes. It just was not the done thing.

"Now it's time for us to go to my home," said the Arab.

Dajekala grew very sad.

"My dear parents, I know I've been born under an unlucky star, but I have one wish. Could you please at least give me Tvalchit'a as part of my dowry?"

Of course the parents could not say no to their unlucky daughter, and they gave her what she asked for – they helped her up on to Tvalchit'a's back. The Arab was leading a horse and said good-bye to her. They also gave her Tvalchit'a's bridle and chain.

After long or short walk, they came to an open field. The Arab took Dajekala off from the horse and said:

"Let's have a rest for a while. The horse must be hungry too."

The woman sat on the grass; the Arab put his head on her knees and in no time at all he started to snore. Now it was quite customary for the Arab not to wake up for a week after he fell asleep. Dajekala is looking at the dark face of the Arab and her eyes are full of tears. Tvalichi'ta is standing nearby and watching her.

"Get up Dajekala, sit on my back, and I will take you to another country," said the horse.

"But what if he wakes up?"

"Put his head slowly on the side; if he wakes up, tell him that your knees got tired. You only need to sit on me and then, even if the whole Arab world follows us they can still never catch up, and so you really should not worry - no need to worry at all."

The woman moved the Arabs head slowly, got up, sat on the horse and Tvalchita flew like the wind. After a long or a short time, they came to another country and the horse said to her:

"Buy a man's clothes and put them on."

Dajekala bought what she was told. She got dressed in men's clothes and looked so great that you could not take your eyes off her.

One day the woman passed the king's palace on her horse. She saw armed soldiers at the gate, went to them and said:

"I want to ask your king something. Could you let me in or take me to him please?"

The soldiers told a servant and the servant told the king. The king ordered the servant to bring the guest in. Dressed in men's clothes, Dajekala was so handsome that the king couldn't take his eyes off her.

"What do you want young man?" The king asked

"I have a little request your majesty! I come from a far away country; and do not have a house or food here. Could you give me shelter for a short time and, in return, I'll work for you."

"Give this young man a home and a stable for his horse, and food and wine as much as they wish," the King said to his servant.

Dajekala was given a small room, and Tvalchita was placed in a warm stable. One week passed, two weeks passed, and a third week too. Now the king had a son the same age as Dajekala, and he got so attached to the guest that he could not even eat without the new arrival.

The queen one day became suspicious that Dajekala was a woman and so she said to her son:

"My son, I think our guest is a woman not a man."

"If she was a woman, then why should she be dressed as a man?"

"If you don't believe me, test her in a wine drinking contest!"

So one day, when the two friends were sitting the garden, the king's son (who was getting more and more suspicious of his friend's true identity with each day that passed) suggested it to her:

"Let's have a wine-drinking contest – you and me!"

The woman was worried and went to her horse for advice on what she should do.

"Why are you so sad my dear owner?" Tvalchit'a asked

"How could I not be worried when the King's son has asked me to compete in drinking contest? What will happen is that I'll get drunk and then they'll find out that I'm really a woman."

"Not to worry my dear. Do as I tell you. After each toast, say to yourself, *I drink but it's Tvalchit'a who gets drunk.* But when you finish the contest, come to me quickly, so that I won't fall over with all that drink inside me and break my legs."

So Dajekala went to the King's son and agreed to take part in the drinking contest. They sat at the table together. The boy lined up six khalada (a liquid measurement of two litres) jugs for himself and he lined up six for his friend. They started to drink.

Dajekala makes a toast and drinks. At the same time she says to herself: *I drink but it's Tvalchit'a who gets drunk*. And they each knocked back all six jugs that way. Then the boy brought even more wine - three more jugs for himself and three more for his friend too. After drinking just one of the extra jugs, the boy got so drunk that he fell asleep at the table. Dajekala straight away got up, took a wet towel with her, and went to the stable. Tvalchi'ta was so drunk that he could hardly stand and was tottering all over the place.So Dajekala dabbed him on his forehead with her wet towel and that is how she managed to help him recover from his ordeal.

The king's son was so exhausted from drinking that he couldn't get up from his bed for several days.

"Mother, I kept telling you that my friend is a man but you wouldn't believe me. So look, you nearly killed me!"

"No my son, I'm still telling you that your friend is a woman dressed in a man's clothes. If you don't believe me, I can force her to confess to it herself."

The King's wife liked Dajekala so much that she wanted her to become her daughter-in-law.

"My child, I know that you're really a woman, so take off those men's clothes and marry my son. And you couldn't find a better place to go to anywhere."

There was no answer to that. So Dajekala took off the men's clothes and married the king's son, and they lived happily together.

Seven months passed and another kingdom then declared war on them. The king started to make preparations, and asked every man who could fight to come forward to help him.

Dajekala was very worried about her husband and her horse.

One day when Dajekala was lovingly stroking her horse,

Tvalchit'a said:

"I know that the king's son will take me into battle with him. But don't let him take either my diamond chain or my bridle. And if, at any time, you should get into trouble, call out my name and I'll be by your side in an instant."

The king's son got ready for battle and prepared Tvalchit'a for it too.

His wife asked him to leave Tvalchit'a's diamond bridle and the chain. But he would not listen and took both with him.

Two months passed and Dajekala gave birth to golden-haired twins - a boy and a girl. The happy king and queen wrote a letter to their son: "You have golden-haired twins. Let us know if you are happy or unhappy to hear this." The letter was given to a fast messenger to deliver to him on the battlefield.

The messenger secured the letter safely in his hat and then set off.

He became very thirsty from all the travelling he had to do, so when he saw a stream, he went to it and drank to quench his thirst. Then he decided to lie down on the grass to have a short rest, but very soon he fell asleep.

The Arab who had married Dajekala saw the messenger sleeping, came up to him, removed the letter poking out from his hat, read it, tore it into small pieces, and wrote another one instead: "Your wife gave a birth to puppies. Let us know if you are happy or unhappy about this." He put the letter back into the messenger's hat and disappeared into the woods.

The messenger woke up, washed his face in the stream, had lunch and left. After a long or a short walk, he found the King's son on the battlefield and delivered the letter he had been entrusted with. The King's son read the letter from his parents: "You have two bastards. Let us know if you are happy or unhappy about this."

Dear god what have I done wrong? I'm young; I'm fighting for my country and looking death in the eye every second. Is this not enough punishment? And, on top of that, you gave me children to be ashamed of - said the boy to himself, and thought about it for a long time. Finally, he wrote back to his parents. "I don't care how beautiful or not my children are; look after them well until my return".

The messenger took the letter, hid it in his hat once again and set off home. At the stream he had another rest and fell asleep again. All of a sudden, the same Arab came, took the letter out of his hat, tore it up into pieces and wrote another one instead: "Heat up the oven for three days and night and then burn the children alive in it because, even if they are golden-haired children, I don't care. And if you don't obey my order, I'll kill you all on my return". The Arab then put the letter back in the same place.

The messenger woke up, washed his face, had a snack and left. After a long or a short walk, he came to the king and gave him the letter. Everyone in the family read the letter one by one, astonished by the words they found: how could he order these beautiful children to be burned alive? They gave the matter a lot of thought, but the letter was from their king and who could possibly go against their king's command? So they started to kindle the fire in preparation, just as they had been instructed to do. Three days and night passed but nobody could throw these beautiful children into the fire, as everyone felt so sorry for them. The whole sky and earth felt pity on Dajekala. All of a sudden, the same cruel Arab arrived in town; he saw loads of people gathered together, approached an old woman standing in the crowd, and asked her:

"Mother, can you tell me why these people are gathered here, and who needs this oven so hot?"

"It's to burn the king's beautiful children in, but nobody wants to do it. The truth is that all of us feel immense pity for them."

"I will throw them into the fire then," said the Arab, approaching the oven.

The wise Tvalchit'a senses that its owner is in a trouble. It is anxious, neighs loudly, but what can it do? For it is attached to a sturdy beech tree with the diamond bridle, and its legs are tied to the diamond chain. But it tries with all its strength to get away and finally manages to breaks the chains, uproot the beech tree out of the ground, and gallop away as fast as possible.

Just when the Arab is about to pick up the children to throw them into the oven, Tvlachi'ta arrives and neighs at him ferociously:

"What are you doing you inhuman bastard?"

The frightened Arab drops the children and tries to run away, but Tvalchit'a is not going to let him off that easily, to be sure. The horse snatches him up with its teeth, and hurls him instead of the children into the red hot oven.

When Dajekala hears what has happened, she rushes to the horse and starts to hug it, kissing each of its eyes, full of relief and joy.

"Take your children with you, and sit on me," said the horse to her dear owner.

How could Dajekala say no to her saviour!

Dajekala climbed up on to the horse's back, taking both her twins with her, put on the bridle, and so they all set off together.

Tvalchit'a flew like the wind. After a long journey, crossing thousands of mountains, they came to an open field where Tvalchit'a stopped.

"Climb down off my back," Tvalchit'a said to its owner.

Dajekala dismounted, and took her two children down off the horse too.

"The time of my death has come," Tvalchit'a started talking to her. "Don't be afraid, don't worry, and don't cry over me. Listen to me instead, and do what I tell you to do: when I die, strip my skin off, cut my flesh into pieces, and then collect up the bones and the pieces of flesh and place them in two separate piles. Take the bones and spread them out on the ground, and they will turn into a high gate. Place two of my hooves here, opposite each other, and they will become the entrance door; then collect up all the pieces of flesh in a basket and scatter them here and there while walking across the middle of the field, then do the same walking back again – that will turn into a town with long wide streets, with shops and restaurants; put my head with yours, my hair towards your feet, cover yourself with my skin, put my other two hooves on different sides of your bed. On that place a marble palace will be built, and you will become the queen and live there."

As soon as Tvalchit'a finished talking, the horse collapsed and died. Dajekala cried a lot, shed bucket loads of tears over her devoted friend, but could not change anything.

When she had cried her fill, and had no more tears left inside her to shed, she got up, stripped the skin off her horse, cut the flesh into pieces, separated the bones and flesh and placed everything in the field, just as she had been told to do. Soon it became dark, time to go to sleep, so they lay down, put Tvlachita's head where their heads were, the horse-hair at their feet, the hooves of the horse on the sides, covered themselves with the skin, and went to sleep.

In the morning when Dajekala wakes up, what does she see! She and her children are sleeping in a luxuriously decorated room, fit for royalty. She could not believe her eyes; she thought it was a dream. Not only that, but smartly dressed servants were now asking her - what would our queen like then?

Dajekala got up and woke her children. The servants laid the table, and whatever a human could possibly wish for was on it. The queen had breakfast and went out afterwards. She looks around her and what can she see! There is a palace in the middle of the garden. All sorts of fruit trees and flowers are growing in the garden, the birds are singing, and cool, crystal clear spring waters are flowing. In front of the palace a very big apply tree grows, and the tree is so tall that it reaches up to the third floor of the palace. There is a high gate exactly where she threw the bones. And where she placed the hooves a big door can be found. As for the pieces of flesh, wide streets now take their place, and on both sides of the streets there are shops, restaurants and taverns.

The town was given a woman's name, because a woman was now the monarch. The news about the woman's town that had suddenly sprung up spread all over the world, and every day thousands of visitors came to see the new town.

When Dajekala's husband returned from battle and found out that his wife and children were missing, he was heartbroken. He did not smile or talk to anyone anymore. Every day his friends did their best to try to cheer him up, but they were unable to.

After some time had passed, one day when the king's son's friends got together to decide how they might possibly be able to cheer him up, the queen came into the room and said:

"Do you know about the town which everyone visits these days? Perhaps you can take my son there and maybe that will help him to forget about his wife and children."

The friends liked the idea, ordered a carriage, persuaded the king's son to go with them, and they all set off together for the town everyone was talking about.

..

After a long or a short journey, they entered the woman's

town. When Dajekala heard about their arrival, she called her golden-haired son and said:

"My son, your father has arrived in that carriage. Go to him and invite him to the palace, but don't tell him who you are."

The child did so happily, after his mother had hidden his golden hair under a silk scarf so that he would not be recognized. He ran to the carriage, stopped it, and said:

"The queen asks you to come to the palace."

The guests said no from the beginning. But the golden-haired boy did not give up:

"You have to come," he said. "It's a tradition in this town - whoever comes to this town, on the first day they have to pay their respects to the queen."

The guests could not say no this time and went with the boy. They were taken to the third floor of the palace. The king's son looked at Dajekala and she looked vaguely familiar to him, but he thought to himself if this was my wife she would have recognised me herself. He then blamed himself "My wife is always in my thoughts and that must be why I imagine that this woman is her".

Dajekala ordered her servants to prepare a delicious lunch for the guests and the lunch was followed by dinner.

"Stay here tonight and tomorrow we will show you around the town," said Dajekala.

The guests enjoyed themselves very much eating and drinking

at Dakelala's grand palace, until they could eat and drink no more.

"Now it's time to take some fresh air," said Dajekal. "I have only one request to make - there is an apple tree with plump juicy apples growing on it in front of the house. Try not to get tempted to pick them."

"How can we touch anything without your permission, our queen?" All the guests replied in one voice, and then they went out.

"This man is your father. Pick one apple and put it in his pocket when he isn't looking, when he goes to bed," said Dajekala to her son.

So the golden-haired boy picked an apple, and when the guests were preparing to go to bed, he managed to do what his mother had told him to.

In the morning, when the guests got up, Dajekala prepared a special breakfast for them. When they finished eating, the queen asked:

"Did any of you pick an apple?"

"Of course not. How could we?" The guests answered, all in one voice.

Dajekala went out, pretended to count all the apples on the tree and then came back.

"My apple tree had ten apples growing on it, and one is missing. One of you must have picked it."

The worried guests looked at each other with surprise.

"It's not difficult to find the person who stole the apple," said Dajekala, and searched the pockets of each guest. She found the apple in her husband's pocket and said to him - "You will be punished in public for what you have done!"

The embarrassed King's son could not say a word, and neither could his friends. But Dajekala could not continue with the lie a moment longer, and so she said;

"Calm down, king's son, you are as innocent as my children were when they were ordered to be burned alive in the oven."

She called her children in, took their silk head scarves off, and stroked them on their golden-haired heads in a display of great affection.

"These are your children. How can any father order children as beautiful as these to be burnt?"
The king's son could not hold control his emotions and he broke down at this point and wept.
"My dear children," he cried out, as he embraced them. Then he embraced his wife and kissed her many times, over and over again.

Then all the guests realised what had happened, congratulated both of them, and a messenger was sent to tell the king about the good news.

The news spread all over the town, and absolutely everyone - young or old, man or woman - came to the palace to celebrate.In the meantime, the King and queen with their nobles and servants arrived, and all of them were soon dancing and singing, along with everyone else in the town.

This time Dajekala herself arranged the wedding. For all the nine days and nights that the celebrations lasted, the sound of singing and dancing were heard from her palace. There were feasts outside in the streets and every passer-by toasted Dajekala and her husband. I was at that wedding and toasted them too and, I have to admit, drank nine q'antshi (horns) of wine in the process.

I left my troubles there
Brought joy here
I left siftings there
And bought flour here

The Brown Girl: A Case of Soul Theft

"The Soul is the noblest part of man, and was given to us by God that we should nobly use it. There is no thing more precious than a human Soul, nor any earthly thing that can be weighed with it. It is worth all the gold that is in the world, and is more precious than the rubies of the kings" (from *The Fisherman and his Soul* by Oscar Wilde).

Soul loss is the term used to describe the way parts of the psyche become detached when we are faced with traumatic situations. In psychological terms, it is known as dissociation and it works as a defence mechanism, a means of displacing unpleasant feelings, impulses or thoughts into the unconscious. In shamanic terms, these split off parts can be found in non-ordinary reality and are only accessible to those familiar with its topography.

Symptoms of soul-loss can include a loss of connection with one's surroundings or even with oneself, memory loss, repetitive negative behaviour patterns or, in the severest case, even coma. Soul retrieval entails the shaman journeying to find the missing parts and then returning them to the client seeking help.

As well as soul-loss, there is also soul-theft, of one shaman's soul by another shaman and also of the souls of ordinary people by evil spirits.

Lewis refers to the former variety:

A favourite and particularly unpleasant trick employed is for one shaman to cause his opponent's spirit ladder to collapse while its owner is holding a séance. The hapless shaman's spirit is then trapped aloft and deprived of the means of returning to his body. Such soul absence, if prolonged, produces illness and may eventually lead to the death of the unfortunate victim (Lewis, 2003, p.145).

What we find in this particular ballad, however, is a case of soul theft carried out by a scorned lover.

At the time this song was collected, many people would still have believed that ill health could be the result of a curse. For example, in 1884, the Bridport news reported the case of a woman suffering from an illness that mystified doctors. She consulted a gipsy wise woman, who told her she had been ill-wished and cured her with counter-magic. In ballads, the term Brown Girl seems to indicate a country girl. Is she despised by her lover as ignorant and unsophisticated? If so, he soon learns, to his cost, that she has unsuspected knowledge (Froome, 2007, p.22).

Stories and ballads transmitted by word of mouth though a community will, in time, develop many variants, because this kind of transmission cannot, by its very nature, produce word-for-word and note-for-note accuracy. Indeed, as part of the creative process, many storytellers and singers deliberately modify the material they learn to suit their interests and styles. It would therefore be naïve to suppose that there is such a thing as the single "authentic" version of any such work and, in any case, it is quite possible that whatever the "original" was ceased to be performed centuries ago. The fact of the matter is that any version can lay an equal claim to authenticity, so long as it is truly from the indigenous community that created it and not the work of an outside editor.

Starting in the 19th century in England, interested people - academics and amateur scholars - started to take note of what was being lost, and there grew various efforts aimed at preserving the music of the people. One such effort was the collection by Francis James Child in the late 19th century of the texts of over three hundred ballads in the English and Scots traditions (called the Child Ballads), and it is from this collection that the variants presented below were taken.

The Brown Girl *(Child 295A) was printed by John White of Newcastle c1780. Child gives two versions, both sent to him by the Reverend Sabine Baring Gould. The B version Baring Gould claimed to have collected from a local singer, but in reality the B version is a splicing of the A version and a well-known broadside ballad that was popular at the time,* Sally and her True love, Billy.

295A: The Brown Girl

295A.1   'I am as brown as brown can be,
My eyes as black as a sloe;
I am as brisk as a nightingale,
And as wilde as any doe.

295A.2   'My love has sent me a love-letter,
Not far from yonder town,
That he could not fancy me,
Because I was so brown.

295A.3   'I sent him his letter back again,
For his love I valu'd not,
Whether that he could fancy me
Or whether he could not.

295A.4   'He sent me his letter back again,
That he lay dangerous sick,
That I might then go speedily
To give him up his faith.'

295A.5   Now you shall hear what love she had
Then for this love-sick man;
She was a whole long summer's day
In a mile a going on.

295A.6   When she came to her love's bed-side,
Where he lay dangerous sick,

She could not for laughing stand
Upright upon her feet.

295A.7   She had a white wand all in her hand,
And smoothd it all on his breast;
'In faith and troth come pardon me,
I hope your soul's at rest.

295A.8   'I'll do as much for my true-love
As other maidens may;
I'll dance and sing on my love's grave
A whole twelvemonth and a day.'

295B: The Brown Girl

295B.1   'I am as brown as brown can be,
And my eyes as black as sloe;
I am as brisk as brisk can be,
And wild as forest doe.

295B.2   'My love he was so high and proud,
His fortune too so high,
He for another fair pretty maid
Me left and passed me by.

295B.3   'Me did he send a love-letter,
He sent it from the town,
Saying no more he loved me,
For that I was so brown.

295B.4   'I sent his letter back again,
Saying his love I valued not,
Whether that he would fancy me,
Whether that he would not.

295B.5   'When that six months were overpassd,
Were overpassd and gone,
Then did my lover, once so bold,
Lie on his bed and groan.

295B.6   'When that six months were overpassd,

Were gone and overpassd,
O then my lover, once so bold,
With love was sick at last.

295B.7　'First sent he for the doctor-man:
'You, doctor, me must cure;
The pains that now do torture me
I can not long endure.'

295B.8　'Next did he send from out the town,
O next did send for me;
He sent for me, the brown, brown girl
Who once his wife should be.

295B.9　'O neer a bit the doctor-man
His sufferings could relieve;
O never an one but the brown, brown girl
Who could his life reprieve.'

295B.10　Now you shall hear what love she had
For this poor love-sick man,
How all one day, a summer's day,
She walked and never ran.

295B.11　When that she came to his bedside,
Where he lay sick and weak,
O then for laughing she could not stand
Upright upon her feet.

295B.12　'You flouted me, you scouted me,
And many another one;
Now the reward is come at last,
For all that you have done.'

295B.13　The rings she took from off her hands,
The rings by two and three:
'O take, O take these golden rings,
By them remember me.'

295B.14　She had a white wand in her hand,
She strake him on the breast:
'My faith and troth I give back to thee,

So may thy soul have rest.'
295B.15   'Prithee,' said he, 'Forget, forget,
Prithee forget, forgive;
O grant me yet a little space,
That I may be well and live.'
295B.16   'O never will I forget, forgive,
So long as I have breath;
I'll dance above your green, green grave
Where you do lie beneath.'

Whether version B is a hoax or not, makes no difference to the fact that this is basically a ballad about soul theft, about a soul that is stolen from the lover who scorned her by the brown girl, as an act of vengeance, and about a soul that is never returned again. Not all shamanic stories have happy outcomes, and although there are rich rewards to be had from embarking on such journeys, they can also be fraught with dangers. And that is what we are reminded of in this tale.

In both versions A and B of the ballad, we learn that the brown girl had a white wand and that she passed it over the body of her ex-lover. So let us now look at the significance of the wand, and at why it might have been incorporated into this tale.

The old English unit of length of 1007 millimetres was called a "wand", and the wand that has survived today as part of folklore may in fact be a rendition of the ancient British length unit. Thus a true wand would be a metre in length and not 30 cm.

In ecclesiastical and formal government ceremonial, special officials may carry a wand of office or staff of office representing their power, and this is a practice of long standing. In Ancient Egypt, for example, priests were depicted with rods. Its age may be even greater, as Stone Age cave paintings show figures holding sticks, which may be symbolic representations of their power. The rod of Moses was a hazel wand (Genesis 30:37) as depicted in catacomb frescoes of the third and fourth centuries, and in classical Greco-Roman mythology the god Hermes/Mercury has a special wand called a caduceus.

In Wicca and Ceremonial magic, practitioners use wands for the channeling of energy. Though traditionally made of wood, they can also consist of metal or crystal. Practitioners usually prune a branch from an Oak, Hazel, or other tree, or may even buy wood from a hardware store, and then carve it and add decorations to personalize it.

There is some scholarly opinion that the magic wand may have its roots as a symbol of the phallus. However, of greater interest to us is that it may also have originated as the drumming stick of a shaman, especially in Central Asia and Siberia, as when using it to bang on his drum or point, to perform religious, healing, and magical ceremonies. In the ballads such as *Allison Gross* and *The Laily Worm and the Machrel of the Sea*, the villainesses use silver wands to transform their victims, and the wand is used in *The Brown Girl* for evil purposes too.

References

Berman, M. (2008) *Soul Loss and the Shamanic Story*, Newcastle: Cambridge Scholars Publishing.

Child, F. J. (1965), *The English and Scottish Popular Ballads*, v 1, New York: Dover Publications.

Froome, J. (2007) *Songs of Witchcraft & Magic*, Boscastle, Cornwall: The Museum of Witchcraft (the booklet that accompanies the recording).

Lewis, I.M. (2003 3rd Edition) *Ecstatic Religion: a study of shamanism and spirit possession*, London: Routledge (first published 1971 by Penguin Books).

Wilde, O. (1997) *The Fisherman and His Soul and Other Fairy Tales*, Bloomsbury Publishing PLC.

Epilogue: A Time for New Beginnings

Aster novi-belgii was introduced from North America into Britain in 1710. In England these plants bloomed at the same time as St Michael's Day was celebrated, the 29th of September, and so they became associated with the festival of Michaelmas and were given its name. Not surprising then, that I should be presented with the flower on the journey I undertook today, in view of the fact that Michael is my name.

As for St. Michael, he is known as one of the Seven Archangels, and his name in Hebrew means, "Who is Like God." A long tradition identifies St. Michael the Archangel as the leader who remained faithful to God, casting Lucifer out of heaven at God's command, and his powerful aid has always been invoked by the Church in times of emergency. The Popes, for example, have constantly called on St. Michael as the special protector of the Church whenever great evils threatened the people. For this reason, St. Michael is especially honoured at Rome, on Monte Gargano, near Foggia, in Italy, and in France on Mont St. Michel in Normandy. The belief is that in times of extreme danger, when the malice of the devil seems triumphant, St. Michael will come to our aid.

The Michaelmas Daisy comes in many colours, from white to pink to purple. An old verse goes:

The Michaelmas Daisies, among dede weeds,
Bloom for St Michael's valorous deeds.
And seems the last of flowers that stood,
Till the feast of St. Simon and St. Jude.

(The Feast of St. Simon and St. Jude is 28th October) An old custom involving Michaelmas Daisies is to pluck off the petals one by one thus: pull a petal while saying ""S/he loves me," then pull off the next while saying "S/he loves me not," and repeat the process until all the petals are gone. The words you recite while pulling off the very last petal from the flower will let you know if your love is requited or not.

The 29th of September is also one of the 4 English "Quarter Days," days which fall around the Equinoxes or Solstices and mark the beginnings of new natural seasons (i.e., Spring, Summer, Autumn, Winter) and which were used in medieval times to mark "quarters" for legal purposes, such as settling debts. The other days like this are: Lady Day (the Feast of the Annunciation) on March 25, the Feast of St. John on June 24, and Christmas on December 25. So it is also a day for new beginnings.

The end of September, when the Feast of St. Michael (Michaelmas) is celebrated, is also a time when the weather is known to change. In Italy, they say "For St. Michael, heat goes into the heavens," an in Ireland, people expect a marked decrease in sickness or disease. The Irish also consider this a lucky day for fishing, for they say "Plenty comes to the boat on Michael's Day". So let us hope that plenty comes to the boat for us today too but, at the same time, we need to remember that as we sow, so shall we reap. In other words, it is in our hands.

"The Michaelmas Daisy often grows in wayside places
With no care at all"
So I have been knowledgeably informed
And I have it in me to explore those very same places
With no cares at all
And to uncover the treasures waiting for me there

nd to celebrate what I find
I have been given a pair of bongo drums to play
It came as quite a surprise, I can tell you,
Even more so when I was also shown
How to dexterously spin the world on one finger

And so to do what brings me my greatest joy
But now for a refreshing cup of tea
Drunk from a porcelain teacup, of course
What else could one want from life?
Surely nothing for what I have been presented with
Is a real silver spoon to put in my mouth
And now to eat from it

Footnotes

1   Despite the criticism now levelled against Eliade's work, without him the current interest in shamanism would probably never have materialized. So instead of dismissing Eliade out of hand as someone who merely popularised various ethnographic reports written by others, by casting a critical eye over what he has to say and by being selective, it is felt there is still a lot of value to be found in his writing and thus justification for referring to it.

2   Eliade's reputation has taken quite a knock in recent years but Rennie's *Reconstructing Eliade: making sense of religion*, based on his doctoral work, is worth reading in this respect as it helps to redress the balance and place his contribution to the study of shamanism in perspective. In this respect, it is also worth pointing out that although Eliade's *Shamanism and Archaic Techniques of Ecstasy*, was not received as a genuine scholarly work when it was first published in 1951, in fact it had never intended to be. Eliade himself makes this clear in his *Journal* when he explains: "I would like it to be read by poets, playwrights, painters... who would benefit more from it than historians of religions", and "my research could be seen as an attempt to rediscover the forgotten sources of literary inspiration" (quoted in Le Manchec, 1991). However, despite Eliade's stated intentions, the effect of the publication was to rehabilitate shamanism, which had up to that point been associated with little more than backwardness and insanity (see Hamayon, 2000).

3   By considering a form of religious practice that would be regarded as a "borderline" case, we can see whether the definition proposed holds water and how it can be applied. In Candomblé both genuine and imitative forms of trance can be found, and it would thus initially seem to fit into the

above definition:

'False trance is a familiar phenomenon in Candomblé, and is known as *equê*, which Taís defined for me as "a type of theatre." The existence of *equê* does not mean that there is no such thing as genuine trance. But it does mean that people who go into trance have considerable room for maneuver' (Wafer, 1991, p.34).

On the other hand, we learn that 'According to the ideology of Candomblé, people cannot control their own spirits. However, parents-of-saint, *ogãs*, and *equedes*, may control the spirits of others, because they have the authority to do so' (Wafer, 1991, p.102). Therefore, based on the definition proposed in this thesis, as the spirits in Candomblé cannot be controlled by the subject at will, it would have to be classified as a form of spirit possession instead.

BOOKS

O is a symbol of the world, of oneness and unity. In different cultures it also means the "eye," symbolizing knowledge and insight. We aim to publish books that are accessible, constructive and that challenge accepted opinion, both that of academia and the "moral majority."

Our books are available in all good English language bookstores worldwide. If you don't see the book on the shelves ask the bookstore to order it for you, quoting the ISBN number and title. Alternatively you can order online (all major online retail sites carry our titles) or contact the distributor in the relevant country, listed on the copyright page.

See our website www.o-books.net for a full list of over 500 titles, growing by 100 a year.

And tune in to myspiritradio.com for our book review radio show, hosted by June-Elleni Laine, where you can listen to the authors discussing their books.

mySpiritRadio